More books by metaphrog:

Louis - The Clown's Last Words
Louis - Lying to Clive
Louis - Red Letter Day
Strange Weather Lately
Vermin
The Maze

More music by hey:

Dreams never die
4 seasons
magnetophone

More music by múm:

Yesterday Was Dramatic - Today Is OK
Please Smile My Noise Bleeds
Finally We Are No One
Summer Make Good

www.metaphrog.com
www.hey-rec.org
www.randomsummer.com
www.fat-cat.co.uk

Voor Sil Niesten.

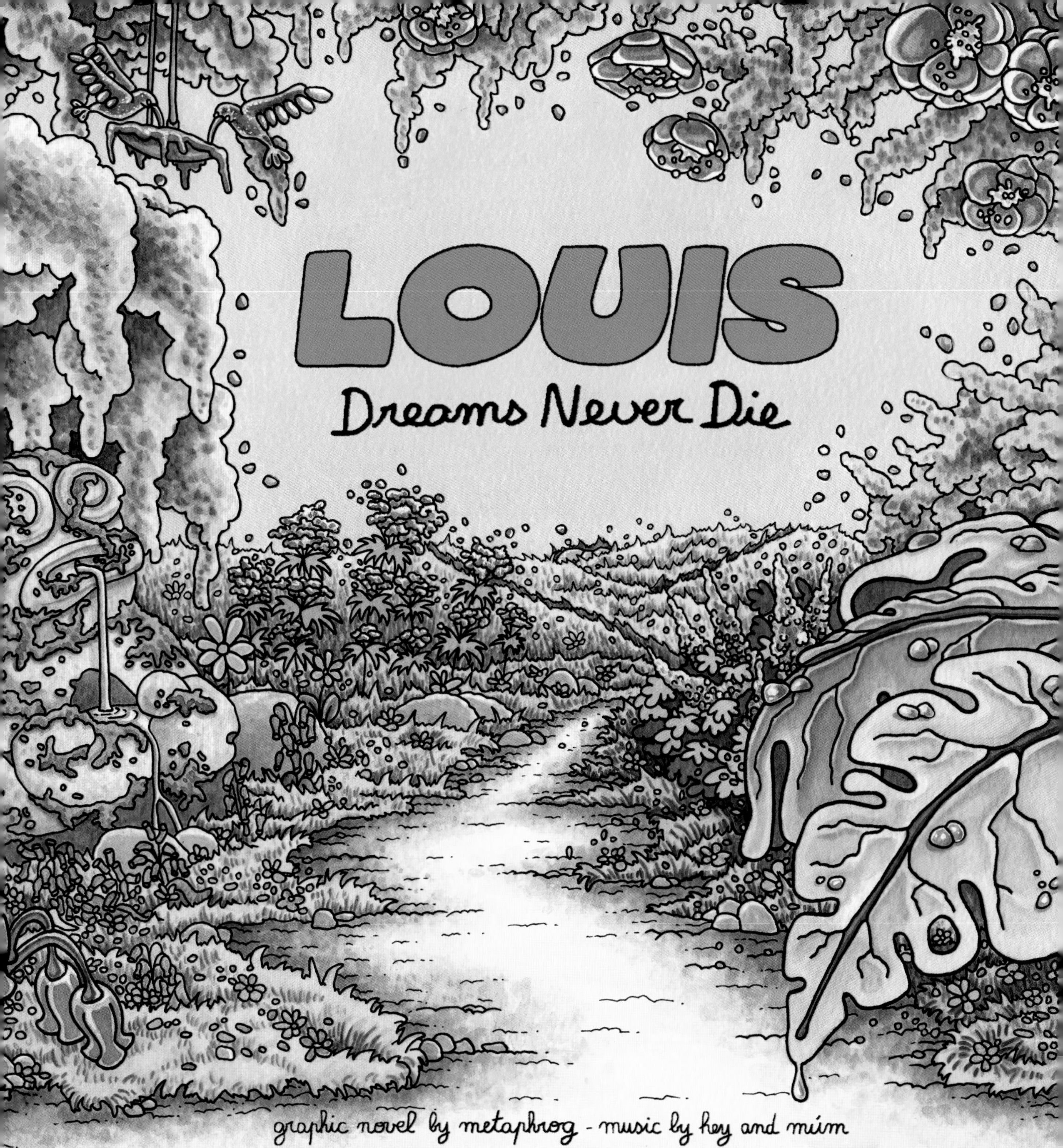
LOUIS
Dreams Never Die

graphic novel by metaphrog - music by hey and múm

This book comes with enhanced cd or vinyl 7":

cd: CDFATPHROG01
1. 'dreams never die to fc' - hey
2. múm version
3. Animation soundtrack - hey / múm
4. 'Louis - Dreams Never Die' animation - metaphrog + soundtrack by hey and múm

vinyl 7": 7FATPHROG01
Side A (Louis with gramophone): 'dreams never die to fc' - hey
Side B (Louis with house): múm version
Animation on: www.louisandfc.com

hey credits: Organ: klaus 'the swimmer' tschabitzer
Legal consultancy: Knut Eigler (Berndorff Rechtsanwälte, Berlin)
Audio mastering: dubplates-mastering.com, Berlin
Manufacturing consultancy: handle with care, Berlin
Animation audio mastering and preloader coding: OlafRupp@gmx.de, Berlin

múm credits: Additional drums, radiator banging and comic book flipping by Samuli Kosminen.
Eiríkur Orri Ólafson blew silly trumpet and clapped his hands to the drums along with el múm.

austro ® mechana

Scottish Arts Council

The publisher acknowleges support from the Scottish Arts Council towards the publication of this title.

fatcat RECORDS

METAPHROG

metaphrog wish to thank hey, múm, and all at FatCat Records.
Thanks to all at Clydeside Press.

Louis - Dreams Never Die

Published by metaphrog in association with FatCat Records.
www.metaphrog.com www.louisandfc.com www.fat-cat.co.uk
Manufactured in the UK.

Original title 'Dreams Never Die' by hey.

ISBN 0954598407

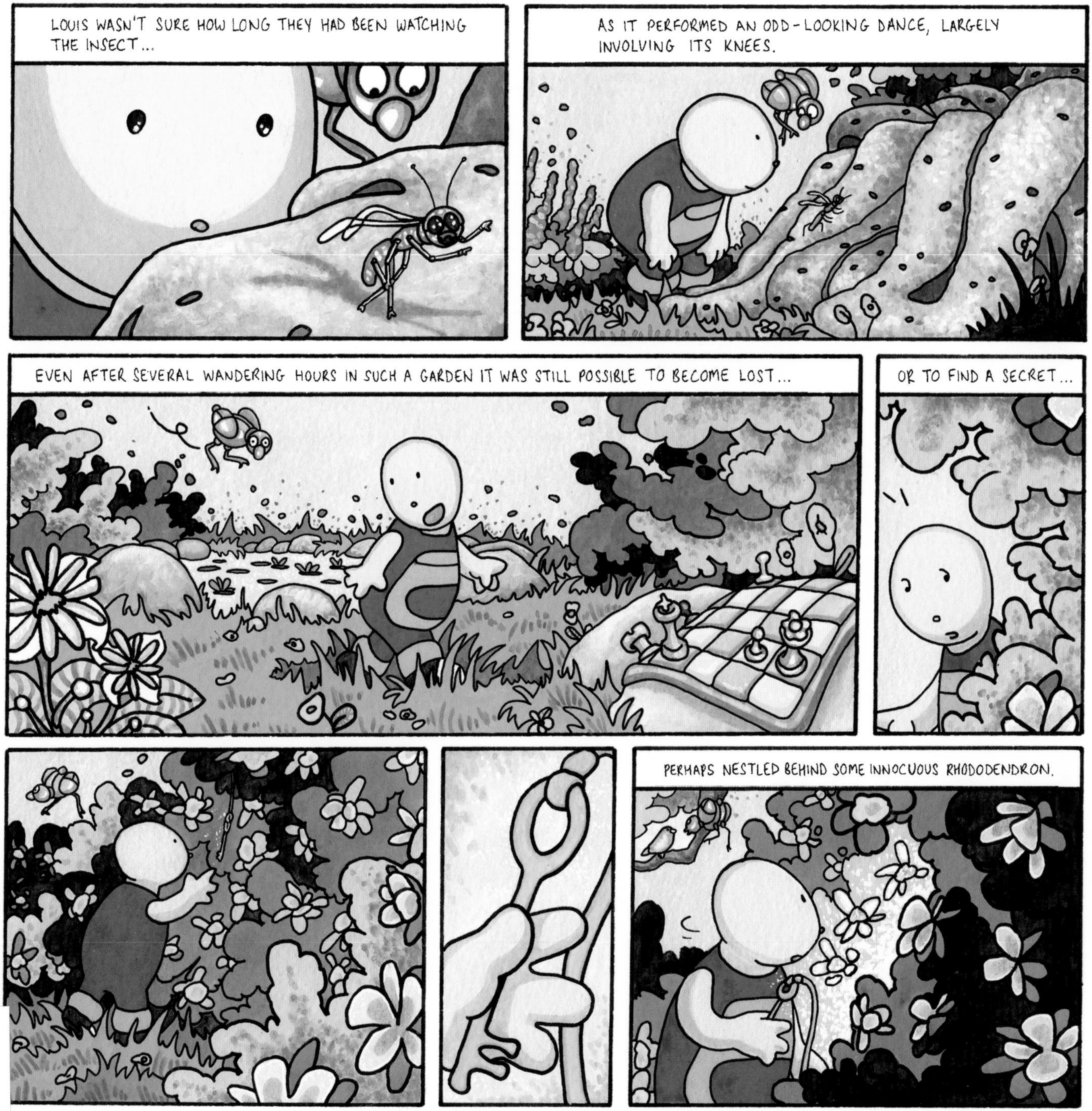
LOUIS WASN'T SURE HOW LONG THEY HAD BEEN WATCHING THE INSECT...
AS IT PERFORMED AN ODD-LOOKING DANCE, LARGELY INVOLVING ITS KNEES.
EVEN AFTER SEVERAL WANDERING HOURS IN SUCH A GARDEN IT WAS STILL POSSIBLE TO BECOME LOST...
OR TO FIND A SECRET...
PERHAPS NESTLED BEHIND SOME INNOCUOUS RHODODENDRON.

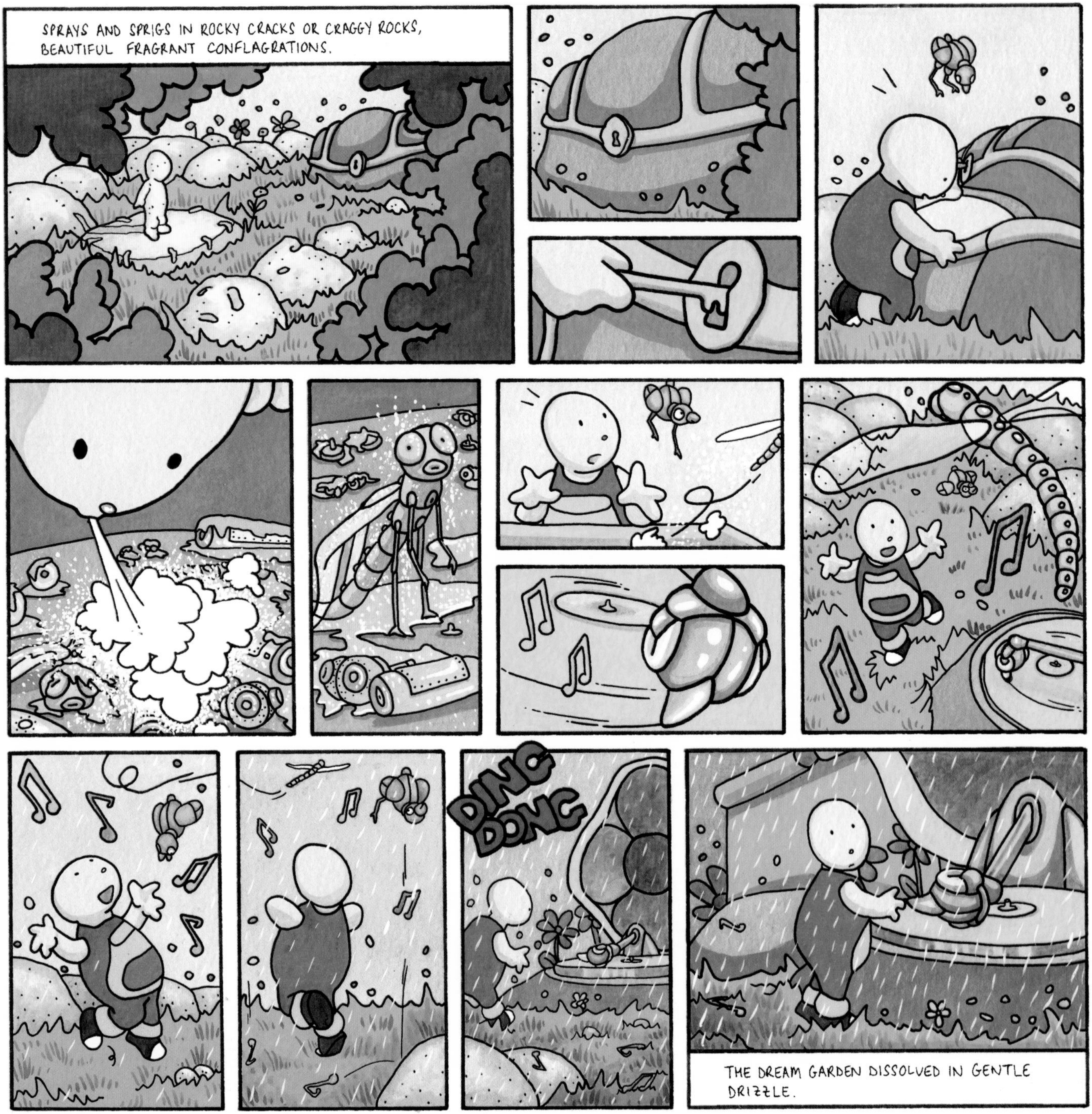
SPRAYS AND SPRIGS IN ROCKY CRACKS OR CRAGGY ROCKS, BEAUTIFUL FRAGRANT CONFLAGRATIONS.
DING DONG
THE DREAM GARDEN DISSOLVED IN GENTLE DRIZZLE.

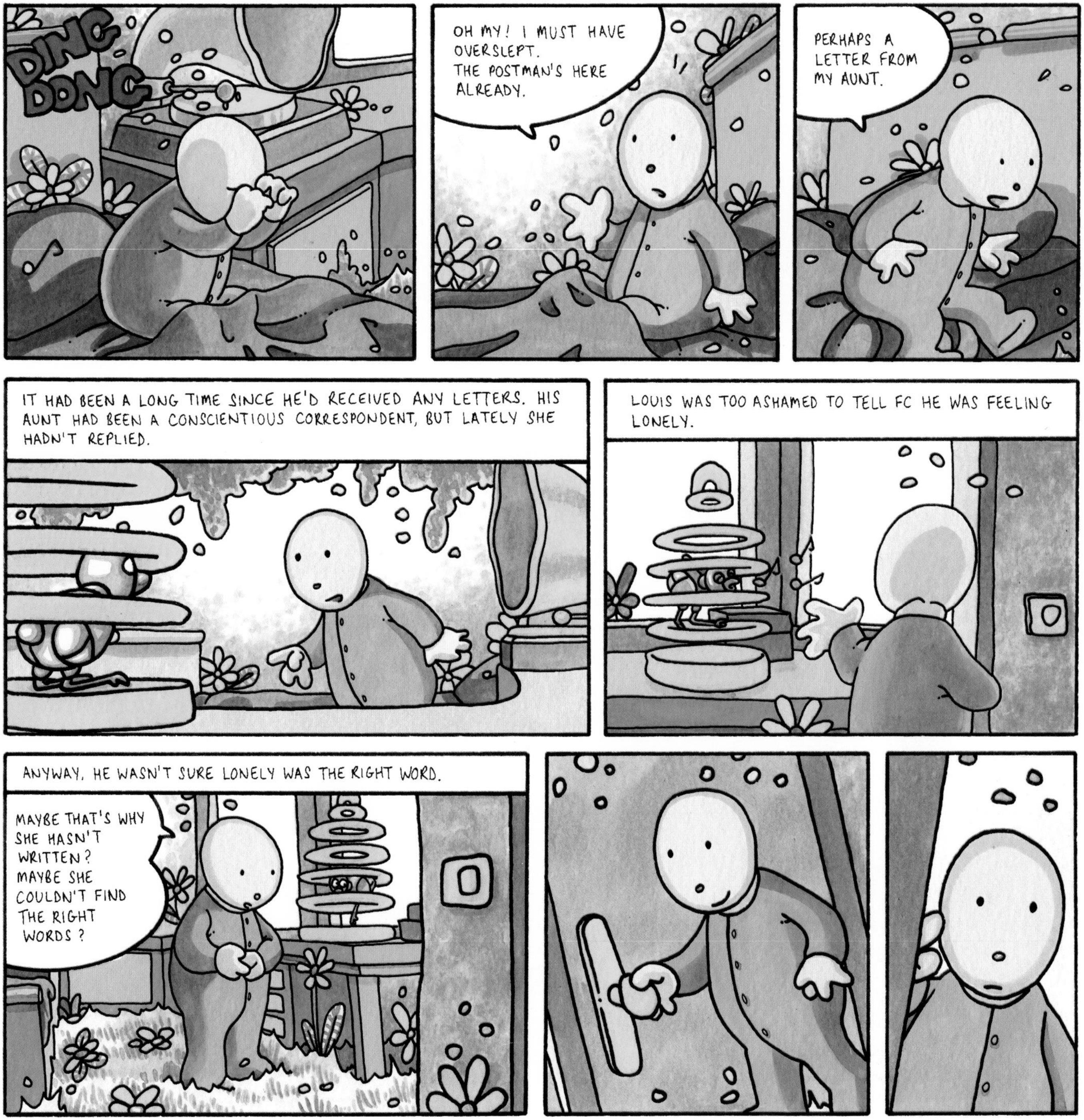
DING DONG
OH MY! I MUST HAVE OVERSLEPT. THE POSTMAN'S HERE ALREADY.
PERHAPS A LETTER FROM MY AUNT.
IT HAD BEEN A LONG TIME SINCE HE'D RECEIVED ANY LETTERS. HIS AUNT HAD BEEN A CONSCIENTIOUS CORRESPONDENT, BUT LATELY SHE HADN'T REPLIED.
LOUIS WAS TOO ASHAMED TO TELL FC HE WAS FEELING LONELY.
ANYWAY, HE WASN'T SURE LONELY WAS THE RIGHT WORD.
MAYBE THAT'S WHY SHE HASN'T WRITTEN? MAYBE SHE COULDN'T FIND THE RIGHT WORDS?

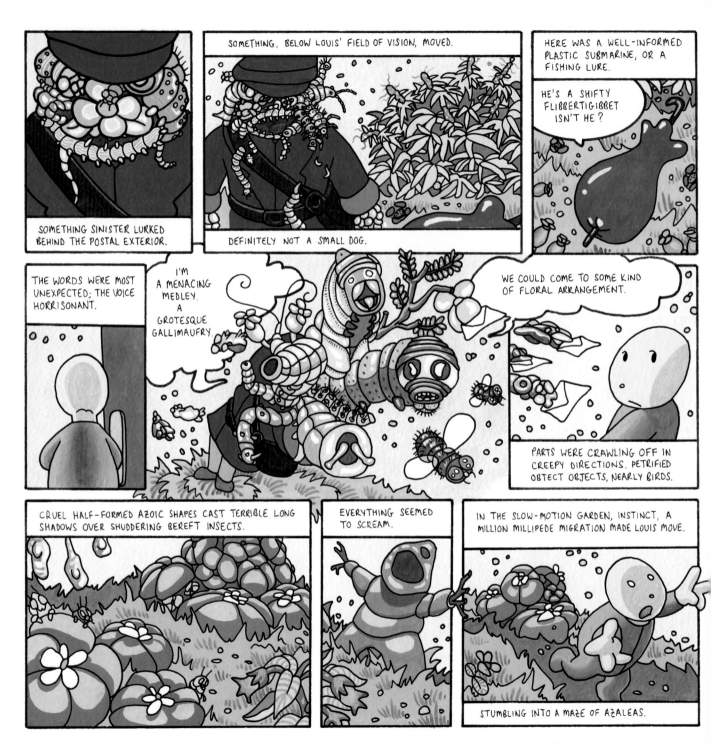

SOMETHING, BELOW LOUIS' FIELD OF VISION, MOVED.

SOMETHING SINISTER LURKED BEHIND THE POSTAL EXTERIOR.

DEFINITELY NOT A SMALL DOG.

HERE WAS A WELL-INFORMED PLASTIC SUBMARINE, OR A FISHING LURE.

HE'S A SHIFTY FLIBBERTIGIBBET ISN'T HE?

THE WORDS WERE MOST UNEXPECTED; THE VOICE HORRISONANT.

I'M A MENACING MEDLEY, A GROTESQUE GALLIMAUFRY.

WE COULD COME TO SOME KIND OF FLORAL ARRANGEMENT.

PARTS WERE CRAWLING OFF IN CREEPY DIRECTIONS. PETRIFIED OBTECT OBJECTS, NEARLY BIRDS.

CRUEL HALF-FORMED AZOIC SHAPES CAST TERRIBLE LONG SHADOWS OVER SHUDDERING BEREFT INSECTS.

EVERYTHING SEEMED TO SCREAM.

IN THE SLOW-MOTION GARDEN, INSTINCT, A MILLION MILLIPEDE MIGRATION MADE LOUIS MOVE.

STUMBLING INTO A MAZE OF AZALEAS.

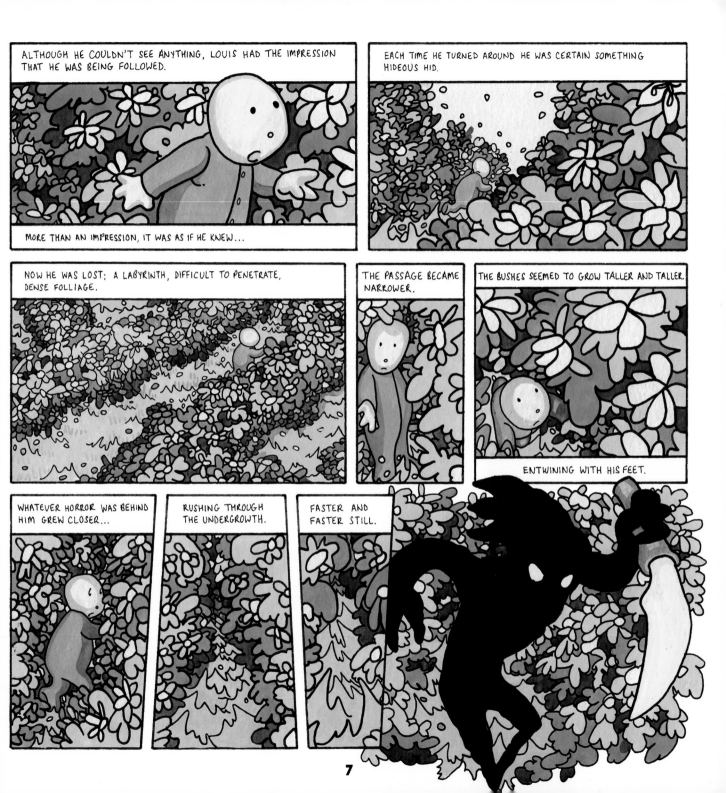

ALTHOUGH HE COULDN'T SEE ANYTHING, LOUIS HAD THE IMPRESSION THAT HE WAS BEING FOLLOWED.

MORE THAN AN IMPRESSION, IT WAS AS IF HE KNEW...

EACH TIME HE TURNED AROUND HE WAS CERTAIN SOMETHING HIDEOUS HID.

NOW HE WAS LOST; A LABYRINTH, DIFFICULT TO PENETRATE, DENSE FOLLIAGE.

THE PASSAGE BECAME NARROWER.

THE BUSHES SEEMED TO GROW TALLER AND TALLER.

ENTWINING WITH HIS FEET.

WHATEVER HORROR WAS BEHIND HIM GREW CLOSER...

RUSHING THROUGH THE UNDERGROWTH.

FASTER AND FASTER STILL.

7

OH MY!

SPECIAL DELIVERY

SPECIAL DELIVERY

LOUIS HAD BEEN DELIGHTED TO FIND A BOX IN THE GARDEN: A SPECIAL DELIVERY.

MORE FOOD BUT ALSO THE MOST REMARKABLE BOOKS.

MORT™
JUST A LITTLE DEATH!

LOUIS HAD BEEN READING UNTIL HIS EYES WEPT.

HE WASN'T SURE IF HE HAD A FAVOURITE BOOK IN THE MYSTERY BOX, BUT THE DICTIONARY WAS A VERITABLE TREASURE TROVE.

SOME KIND OF WORD DREAM.

MORT™
JUST A LITTLE DEATH

STRANGE TUMBLING WORDS...

3120

8

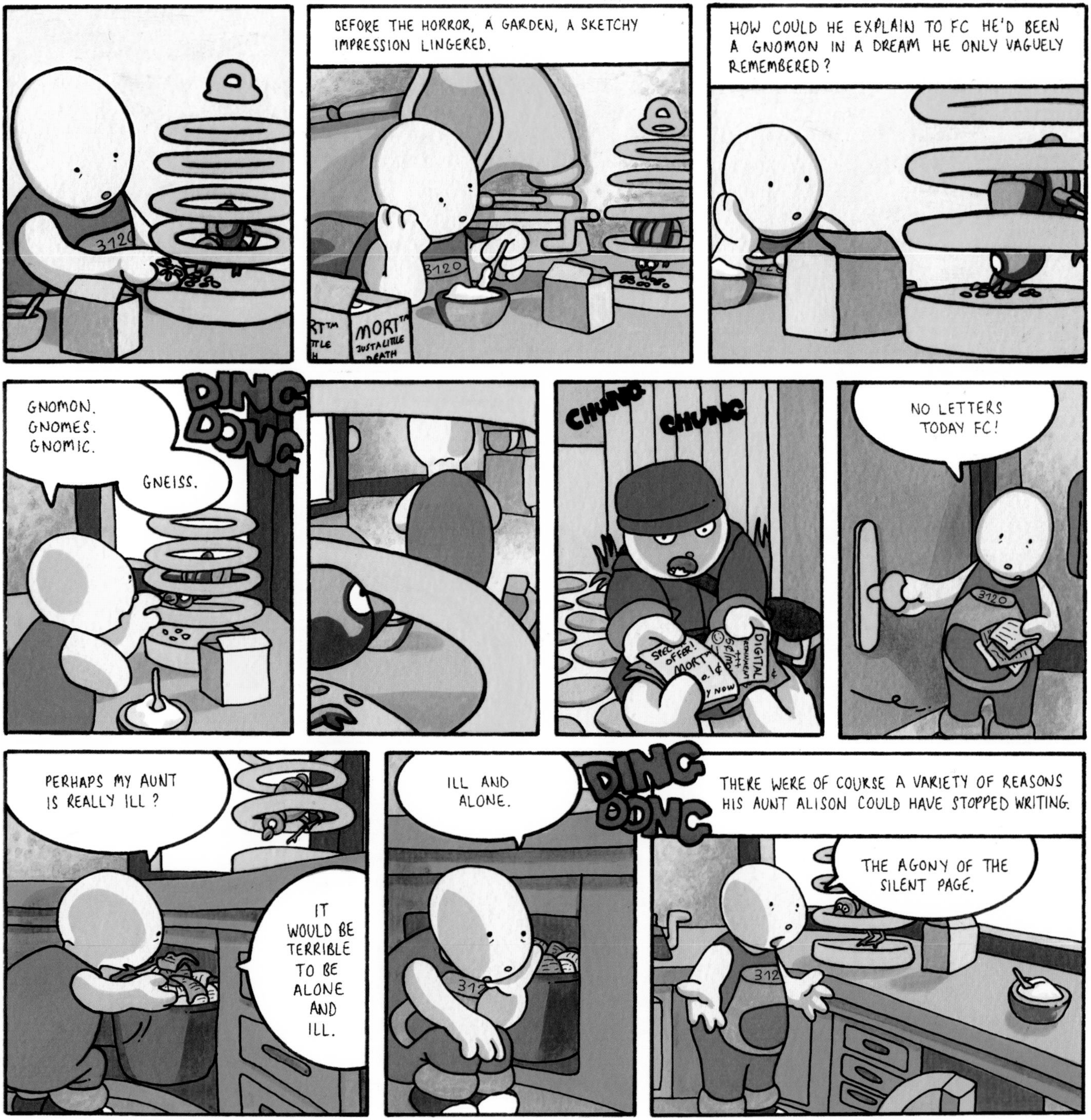
BEFORE THE HORROR, A GARDEN, A SKETCHY IMPRESSION LINGERED.
MORT™ JUST A LITTLE DEATH
HOW COULD HE EXPLAIN TO FC HE'D BEEN A GNOMON IN A DREAM HE ONLY VAGUELY REMEMBERED?
GNOMON. GNOMES. GNOMIC.
GNEISS.
DING DONG
CHUNG
CHUNG
SPECIAL OFFER! MORT™ 0.1¢
DIGITAL
NO LETTERS TODAY FC!
PERHAPS MY AUNT IS REALLY ILL?
IT WOULD BE TERRIBLE TO BE ALONE AND ILL.
ILL AND ALONE.
DING DONG
THERE WERE OF COURSE A VARIETY OF REASONS HIS AUNT ALISON COULD HAVE STOPPED WRITING.
THE AGONY OF THE SILENT PAGE.

MORNING ACTIVITY HAD PASSED IN A FUGUE, AFTER HIS NIGHT TERROR HE HAD FELT REALLY TIRED, ALMOST FATIGUED.

POOT!

LOUIS WONDERED WHEN HE HAD PROGRESSED TO PINEAPPLES.

THERE'S MORE TO FRUIT THAN MEETS THE EYE.

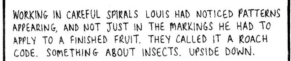

WORKING IN CAREFUL SPIRALS LOUIS HAD NOTICED PATTERNS APPEARING, AND NOT JUST IN THE MARKINGS HE HAD TO APPLY TO A FINISHED FRUIT. THEY CALLED IT A ROACH CODE. SOMETHING ABOUT INSECTS. UPSIDE DOWN.

LOUIS HAD OFTEN WONDERED ABOUT THAT.

THEY SAID PINEAPPLES WERE AN EXOTIC FRUIT. DIFFICULT TO PRODUCE. REQUIRING DEXTERITY.

FRUIT STAINED IF THE SPILLAGE WASN'T WIPED RIGHT AWAY, MARKED THE VERY TEXTURE OF A FABRIC, GOT RIGHT INTO THE WARP AND WEFT.

HOW LONG HAD HE KNOWN HE HAD AN AUNT?

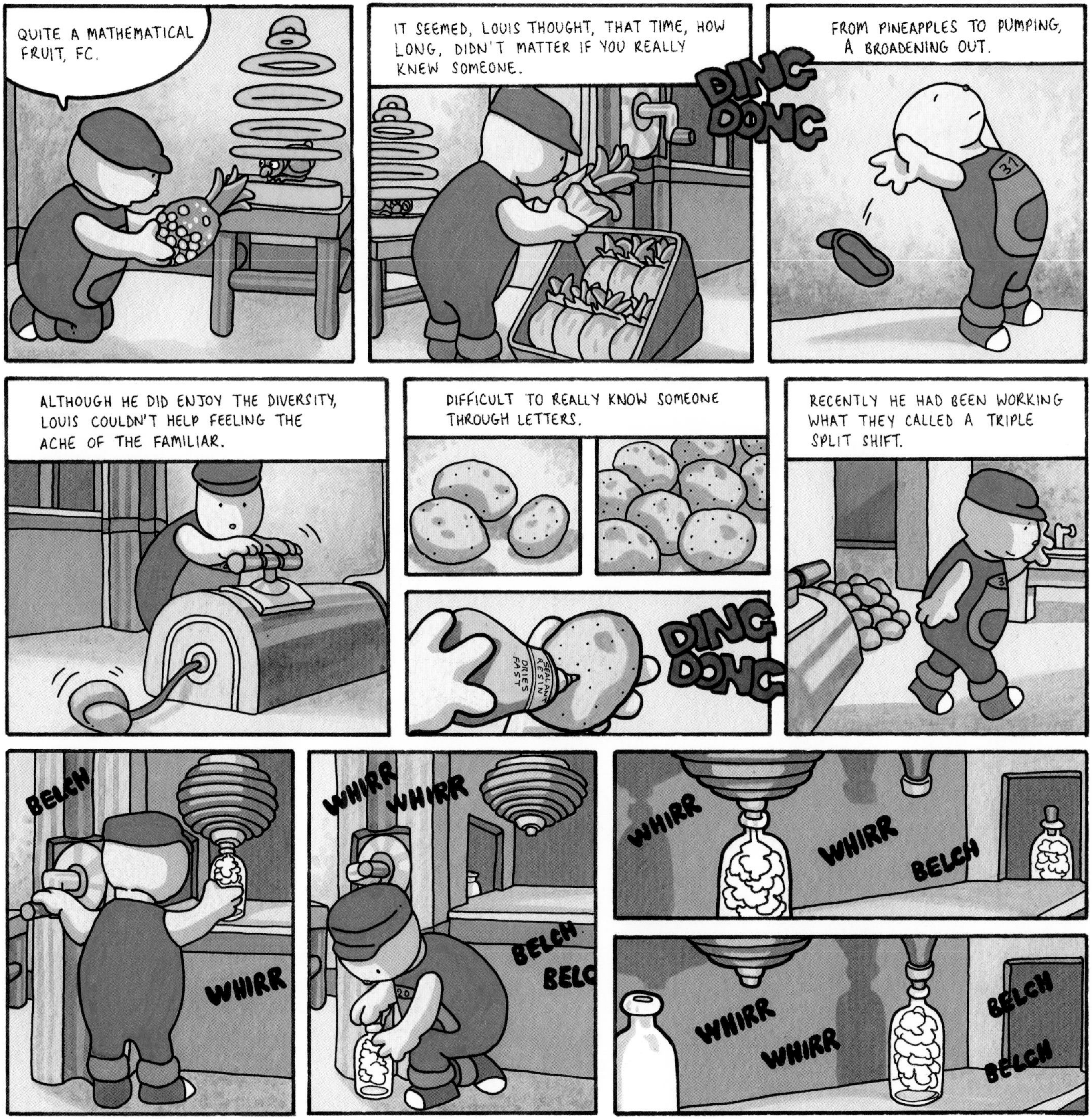
QUITE A MATHEMATICAL FRUIT, FC.
IT SEEMED, LOUIS THOUGHT, THAT TIME, HOW LONG, DIDN'T MATTER IF YOU REALLY KNEW SOMEONE.
DING DONG
FROM PINEAPPLES TO PUMPING, A BROADENING OUT.
31
ALTHOUGH HE DID ENJOY THE DIVERSITY, LOUIS COULDN'T HELP FEELING THE ACHE OF THE FAMILIAR.
DIFFICULT TO REALLY KNOW SOMEONE THROUGH LETTERS.
SEALANT RESIN DRIES FAST
DING DONG
RECENTLY HE HAD BEEN WORKING WHAT THEY CALLED A TRIPLE SPLIT SHIFT.
BELCH
WHIRR
WHIRR WHIRR
BELCH
BELC
WHIRR
WHIRR
BELCH
WHIRR
WHIRR
BELCH
BELCH

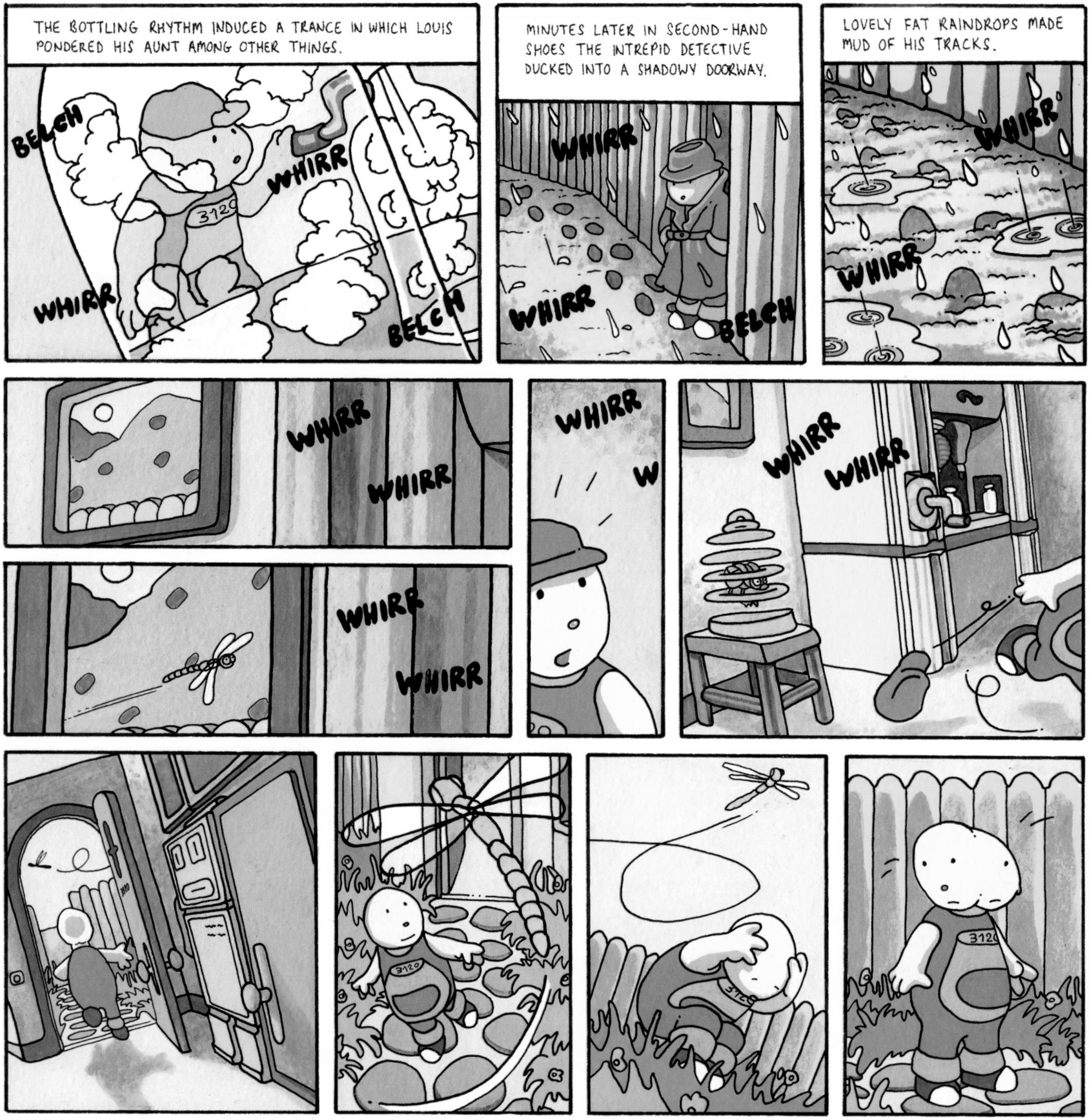
THE BOTTLING RHYTHM INDUCED A TRANCE IN WHICH LOUIS PONDERED HIS AUNT AMONG OTHER THINGS.
BELCH
WHIRR
3120
WHIRR
BELCH
MINUTES LATER IN SECOND-HAND SHOES THE INTREPID DETECTIVE DUCKED INTO A SHADOWY DOORWAY.
WHIRR
WHIRR
BELCH
LOVELY FAT RAINDROPS MADE MUD OF HIS TRACKS.
WHIRR
WHIRR
WHIRR
WHIRR
WHIRR
WHIRR
WHIRR
W
WHIRR
WHIRR
3120
3120
3120

DRAGONFLIES ARE FIERCELY TERRITORIAL.

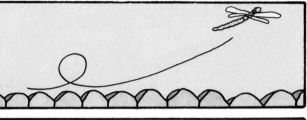

WHAT A WONDEROUS FLYING-MACHINE FC!

PAINFULLY, LOUIS REALISED SOMETHING.

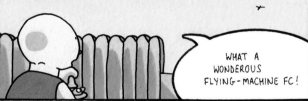

YOU CAN HURT SOMEONE WITHOUT MEANING TO.

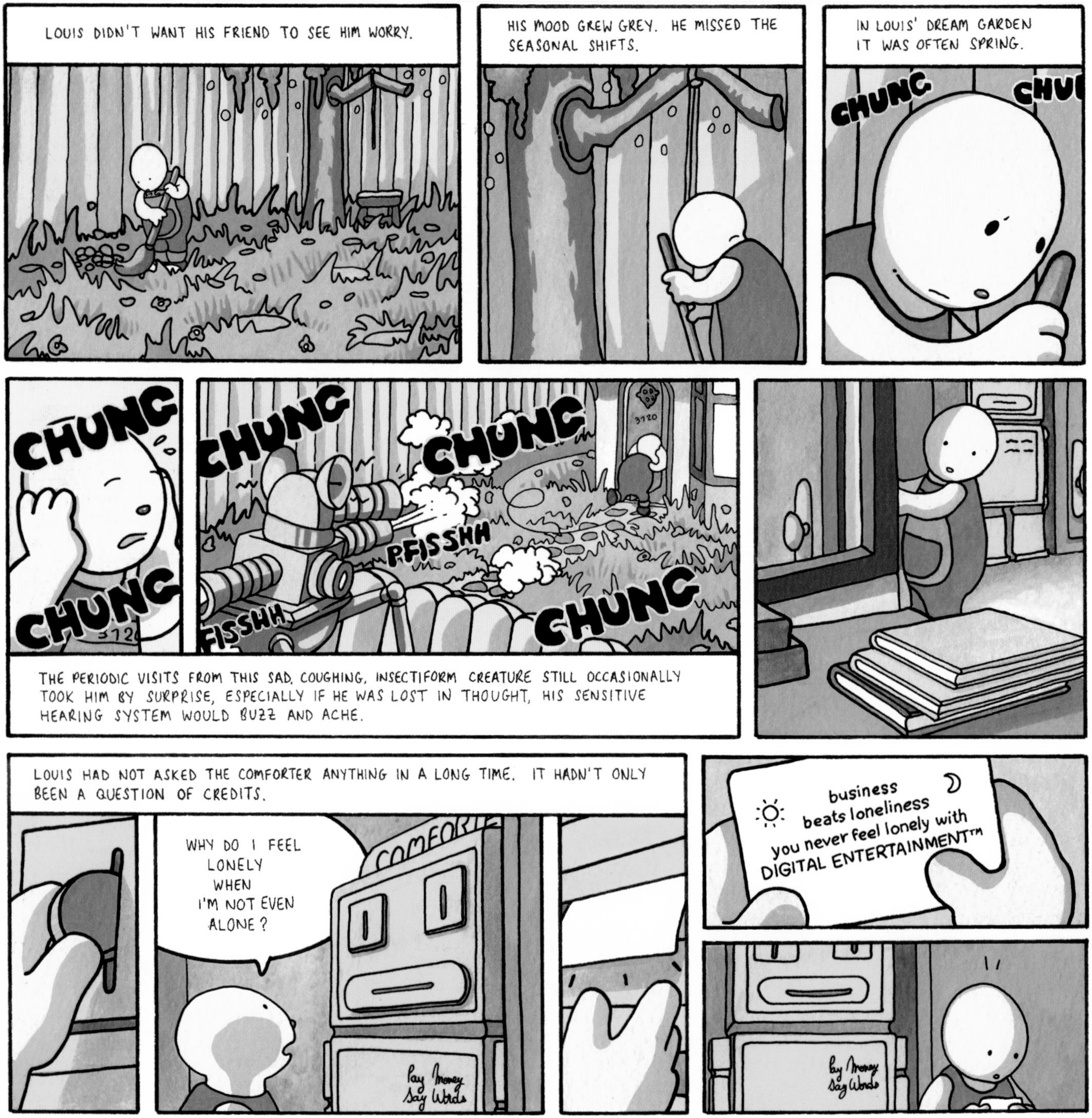
LOUIS DIDN'T WANT HIS FRIEND TO SEE HIM WORRY.
HIS MOOD GREW GREY. HE MISSED THE SEASONAL SHIFTS.
IN LOUIS' DREAM GARDEN IT WAS OFTEN SPRING.
CHUNG
CHUNG
CHUNG
CHUNG
CHUNG
CHUNG
3120
PFISSHH
FISSHH
CHUNG
THE PERIODIC VISITS FROM THIS SAD, COUGHING, INSECTIFORM CREATURE STILL OCCASIONALLY TOOK HIM BY SURPRISE, ESPECIALLY IF HE WAS LOST IN THOUGHT, HIS SENSITIVE HEARING SYSTEM WOULD BUZZ AND ACHE.
LOUIS HAD NOT ASKED THE COMFORTER ANYTHING IN A LONG TIME. IT HADN'T ONLY BEEN A QUESTION OF CREDITS.
WHY DO I FEEL LONELY WHEN I'M NOT EVEN ALONE?
Pay Money Say Words
business beats loneliness
you never feel lonely with DIGITAL ENTERTAINMENT™
Pay Money Say Words

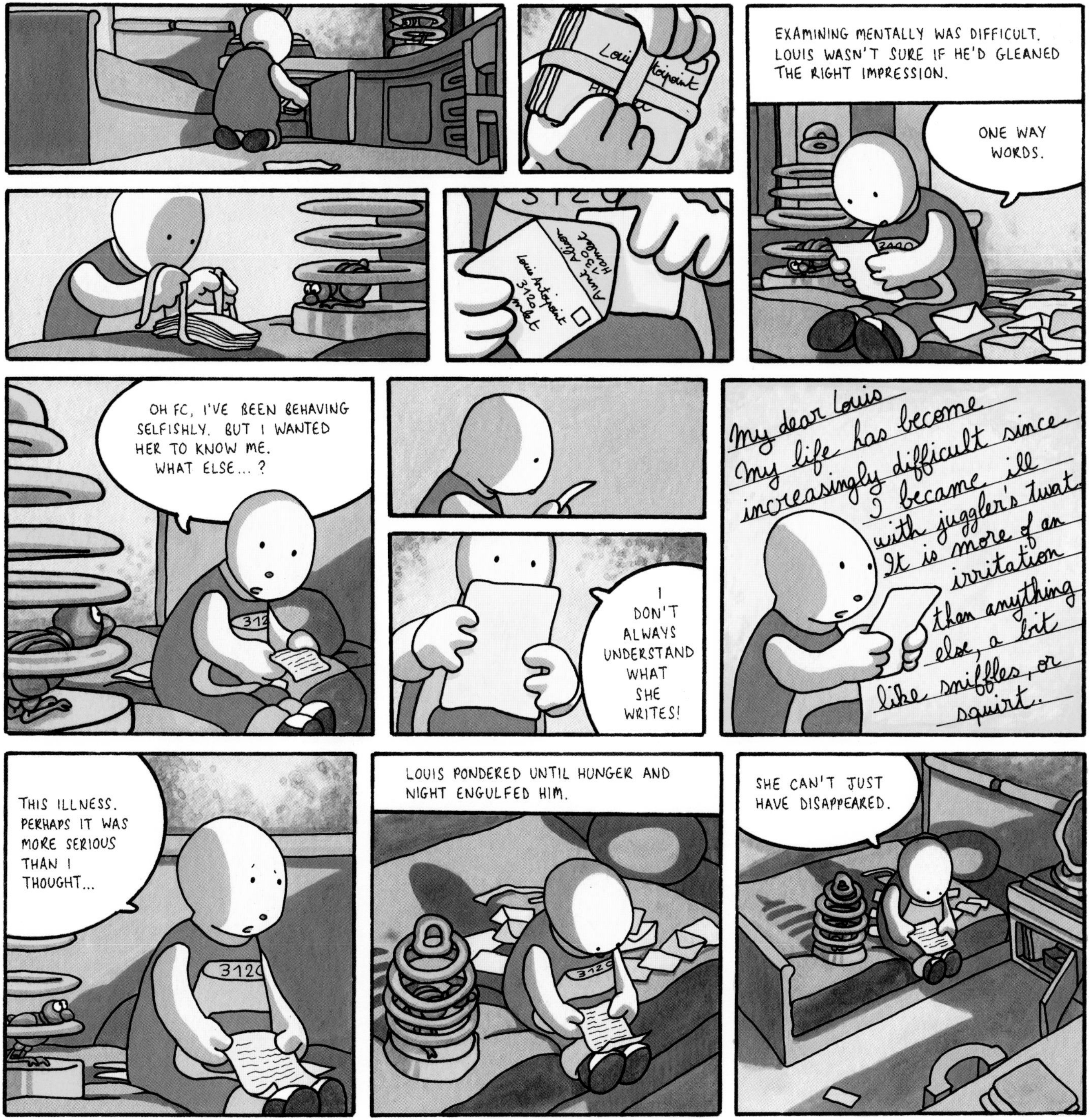

EXAMINING MENTALLY WAS DIFFICULT. LOUIS WASN'T SURE IF HE'D GLEANED THE RIGHT IMPRESSION.
ONE WAY WORDS.
OH FC, I'VE BEEN BEHAVING SELFISHLY. BUT I WANTED HER TO KNOW ME. WHAT ELSE... ?
I DON'T ALWAYS UNDERSTAND WHAT SHE WRITES!
My dear Louis
My life has become increasingly difficult since I became ill with juggler's twat. It is more of an irritation than anything else, a bit like sniffles, or squirt.
THIS ILLNESS. PERHAPS IT WAS MORE SERIOUS THAN I THOUGHT...
LOUIS PONDERED UNTIL HUNGER AND NIGHT ENGULFED HIM.
SHE CAN'T JUST HAVE DISAPPEARED.

MAGIC.

HA HA
HA HA
HA

ALTHOUGH YOU CAN'T SEE THE STARS IN THE SKY, YOU FEEL SAFE IN THE THOUGHT THEY LIGHT YOUR SLEEP.

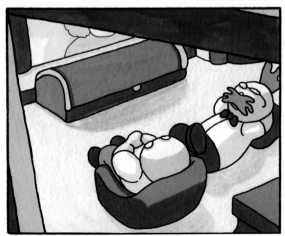

16

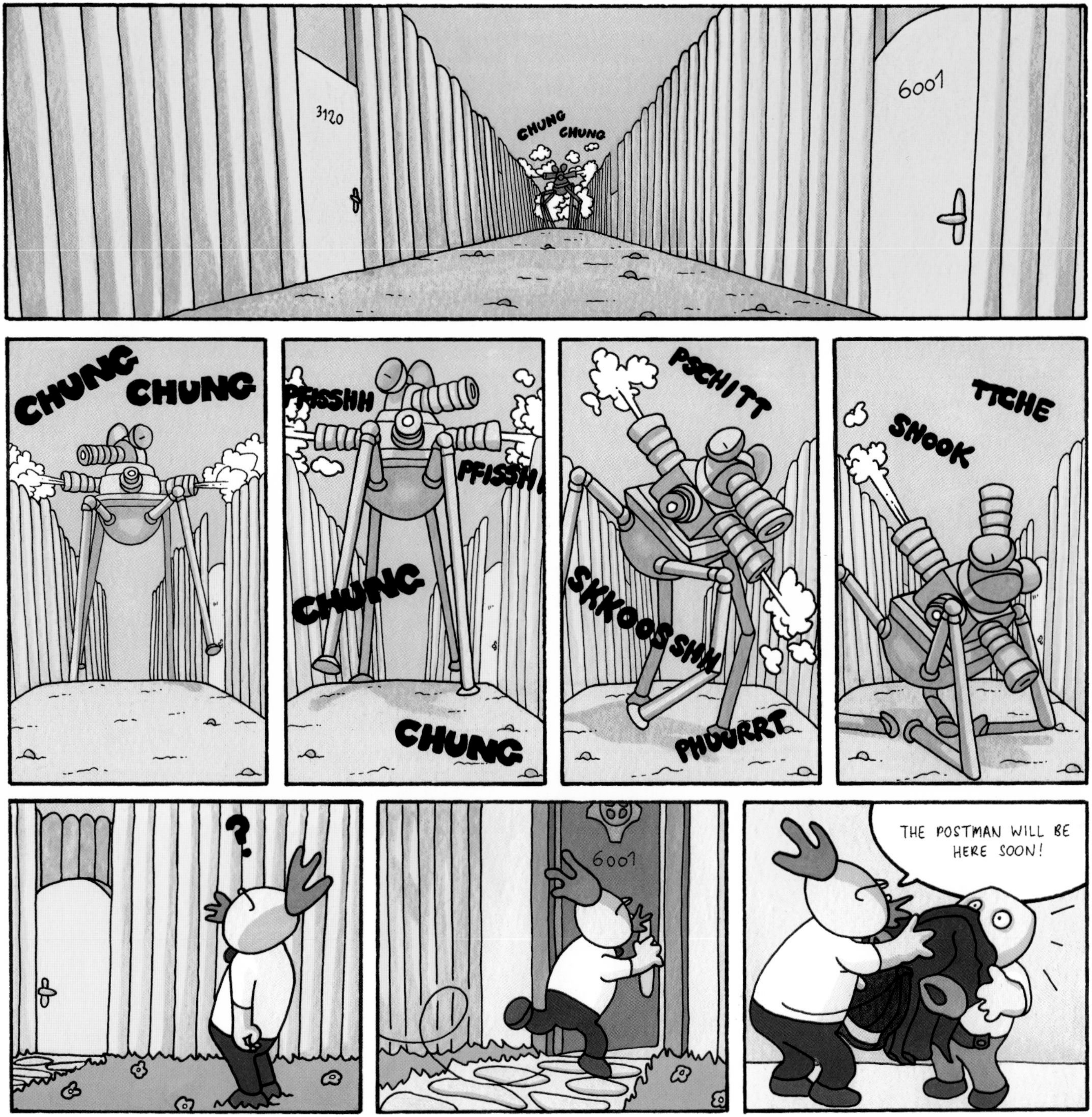
3120
6001
CHUNG
CHUNG
CHUNG
CHUNG
PFISSHH
PFISSHH
CHUNG
CHUNG
PSCHITT
SKKOOSSHH
PHUURRT
TICHE
SNOOK
?
6001
THE POSTMAN WILL BE HERE SOON!

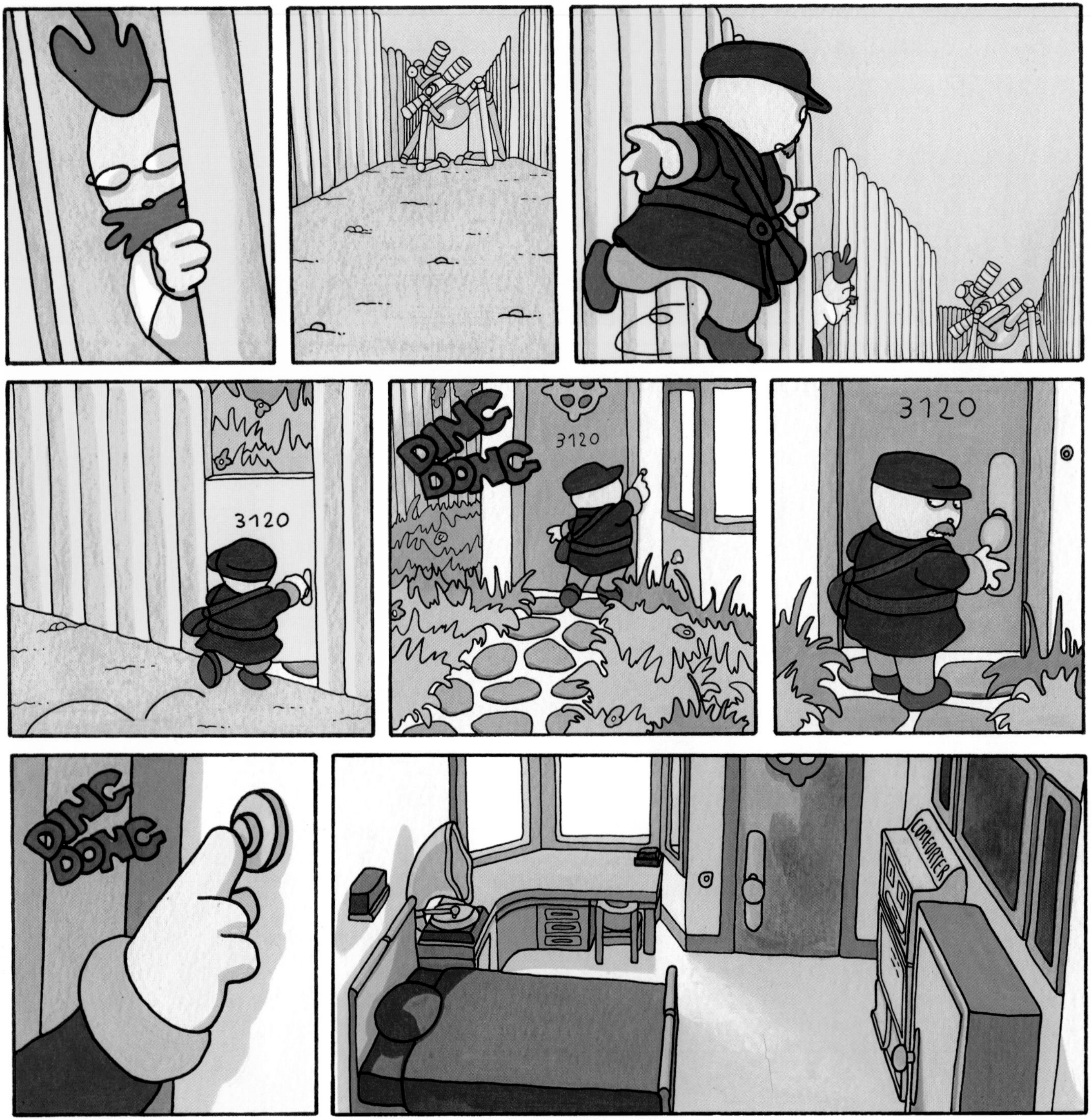
3120
DING DONG
3120
3120
DING DONG
COMFORTER

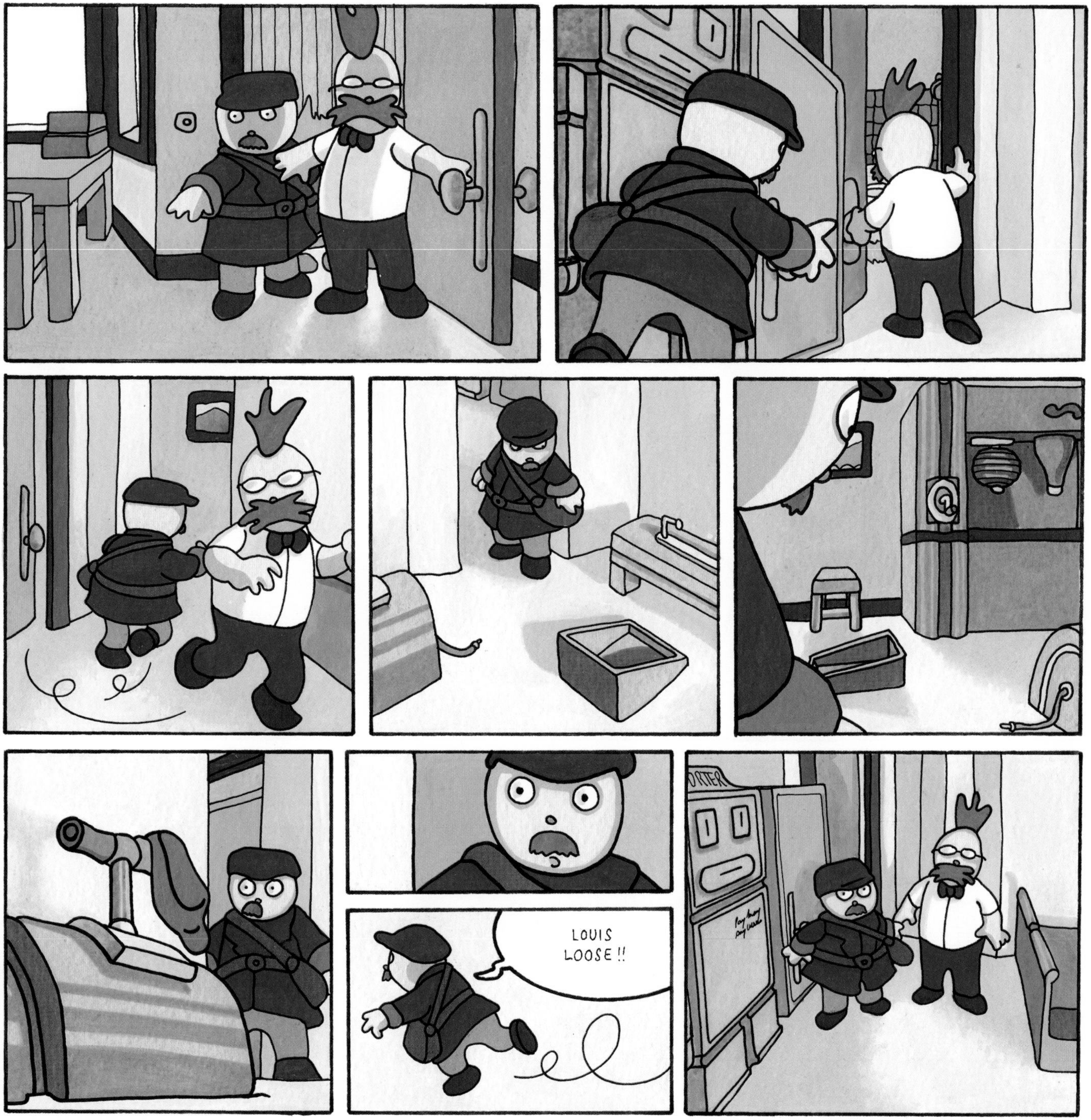
LOUIS LOOSE !!

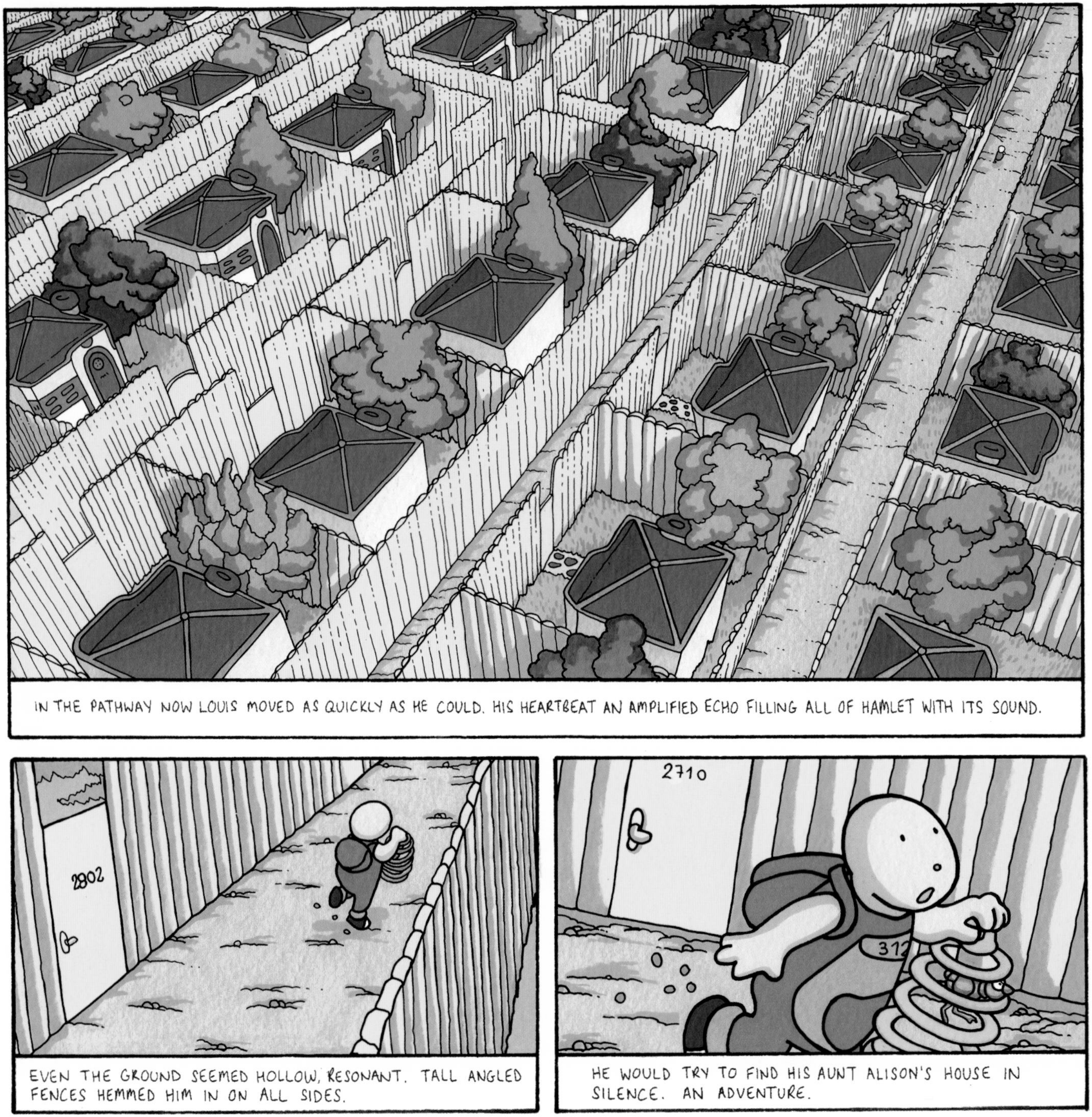
IN THE PATHWAY NOW LOUIS MOVED AS QUICKLY AS HE COULD. HIS HEARTBEAT AN AMPLIFIED ECHO FILLING ALL OF HAMLET WITH ITS SOUND.
2802
EVEN THE GROUND SEEMED HOLLOW, RESONANT. TALL ANGLED FENCES HEMMED HIM IN ON ALL SIDES.
2710
312
HE WOULD TRY TO FIND HIS AUNT ALISON'S HOUSE IN SILENCE. AN ADVENTURE.

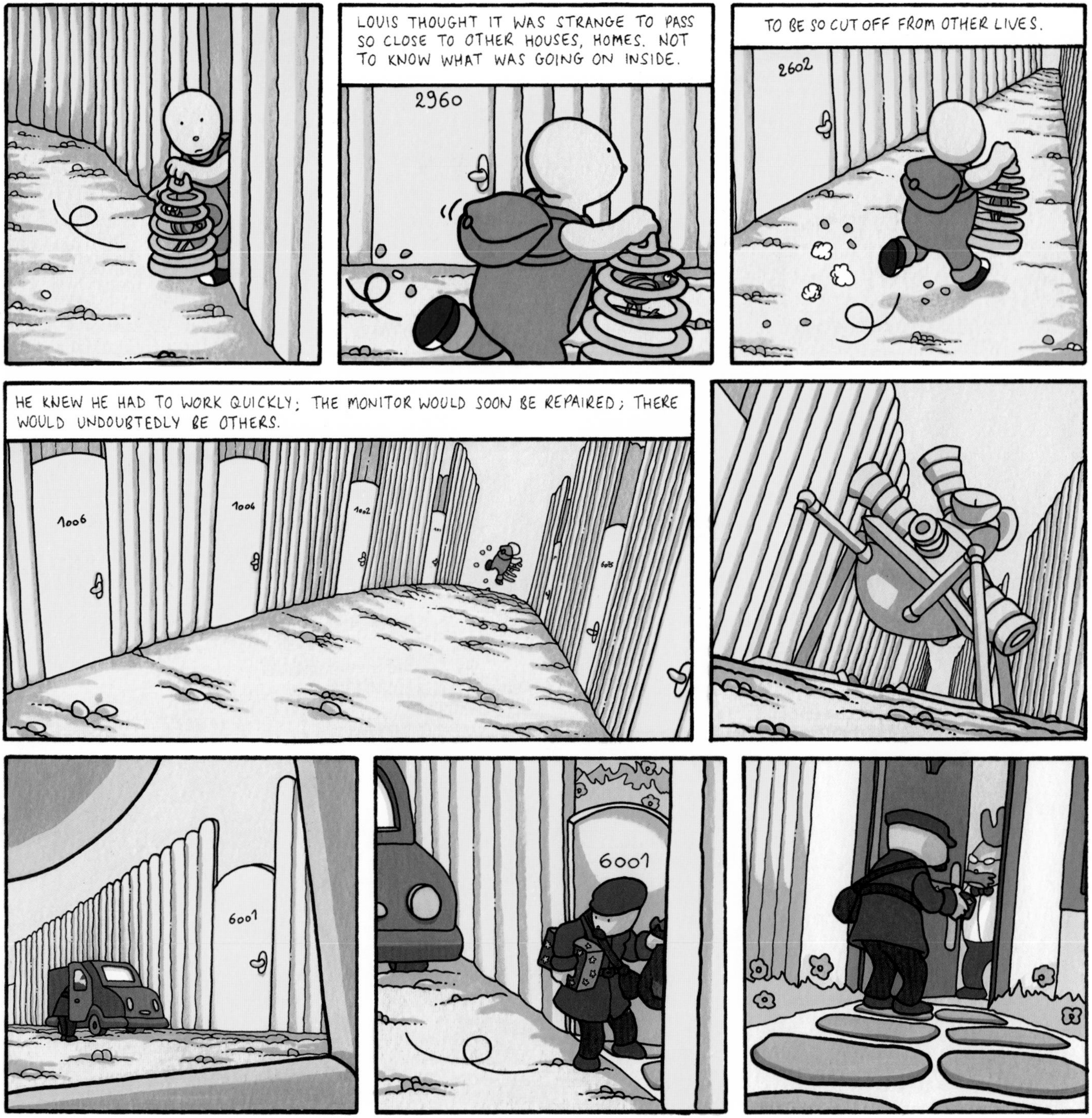
LOUIS THOUGHT IT WAS STRANGE TO PASS SO CLOSE TO OTHER HOUSES, HOMES. NOT TO KNOW WHAT WAS GOING ON INSIDE.
2960
TO BE SO CUT OFF FROM OTHER LIVES.
2602
HE KNEW HE HAD TO WORK QUICKLY: THE MONITOR WOULD SOON BE REPAIRED; THERE WOULD UNDOUBTEDLY BE OTHERS.
1006
1006
6001
6001

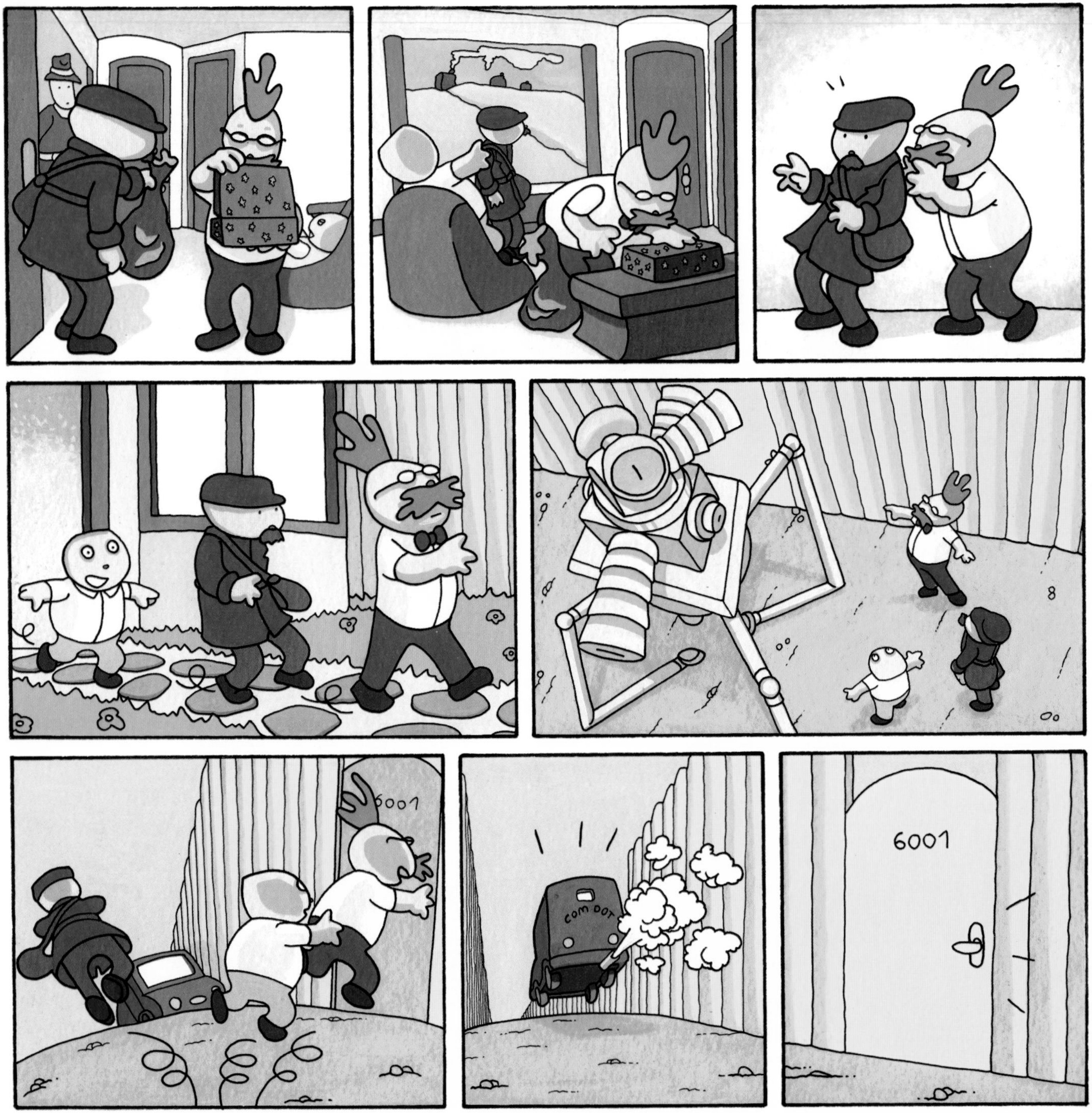
6001
COM DOT
6001

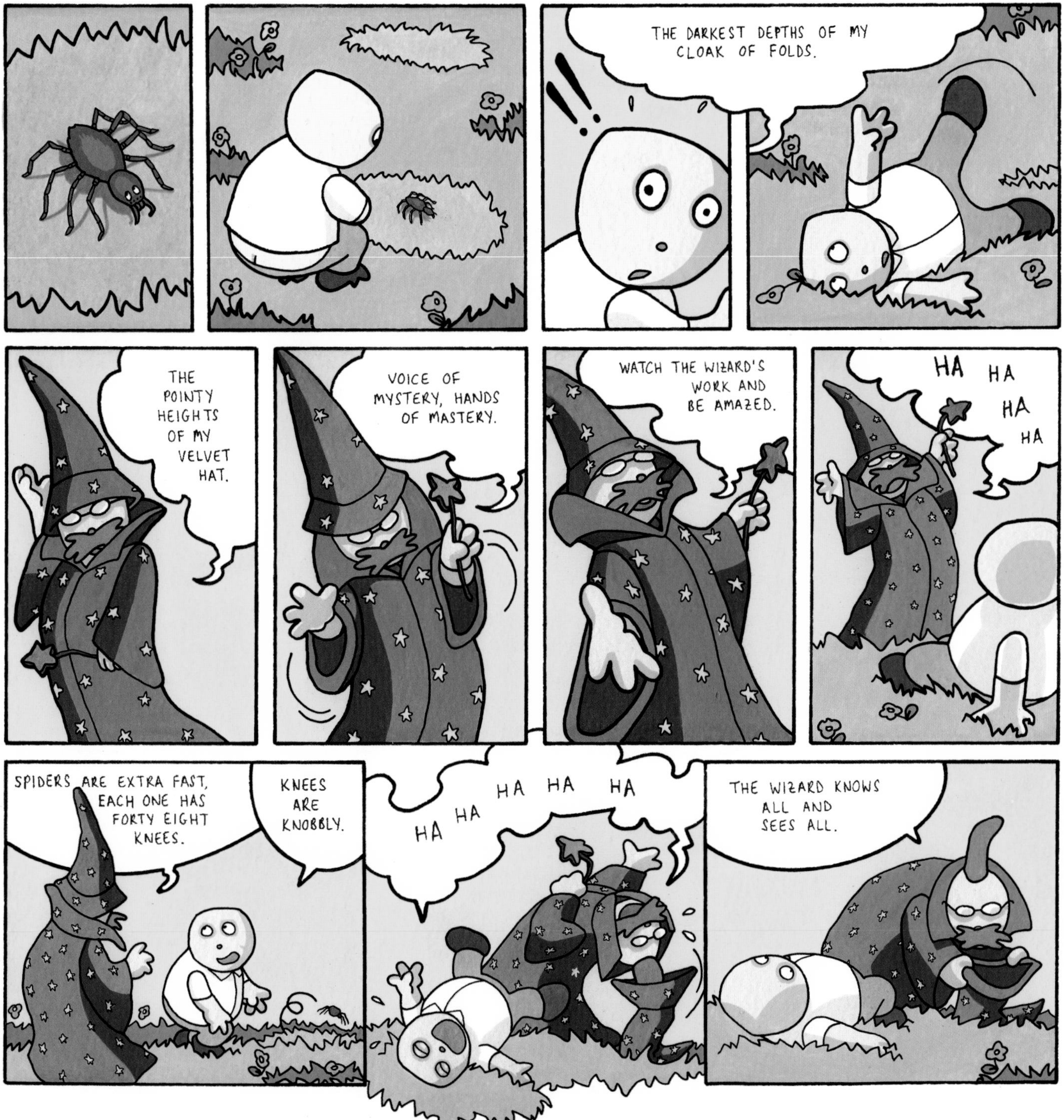
THE DARKEST DEPTHS OF MY CLOAK OF FOLDS.
!!
THE POINTY HEIGHTS OF MY VELVET HAT.
VOICE OF MYSTERY, HANDS OF MASTERY.
WATCH THE WIZARD'S WORK AND BE AMAZED.
HA HA HA HA
SPIDERS ARE EXTRA FAST, EACH ONE HAS FORTY EIGHT KNEES.
KNEES ARE KNOBBLY.
HA HA HA HA HA
THE WIZARD KNOWS ALL AND SEES ALL.

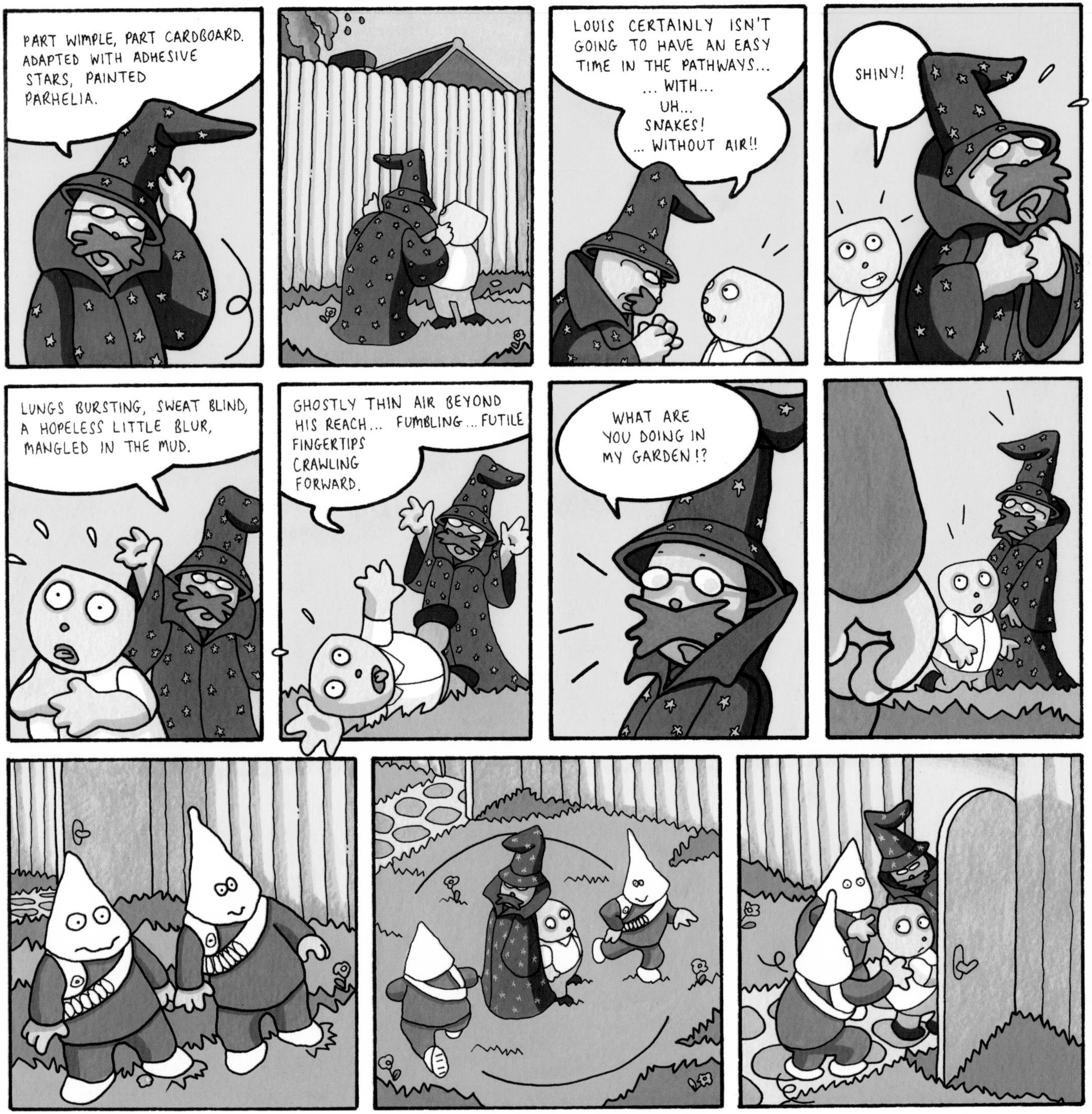
PART WIMPLE, PART CARDBOARD. ADAPTED WITH ADHESIVE STARS, PAINTED PARHELIA.
LOUIS CERTAINLY ISN'T GOING TO HAVE AN EASY TIME IN THE PATHWAYS... ... WITH... UH... SNAKES! ... WITHOUT AIR!!
SHINY!
LUNGS BURSTING, SWEAT BLIND, A HOPELESS LITTLE BLUR, MANGLED IN THE MUD.
GHOSTLY THIN AIR BEYOND HIS REACH... FUMBLING... FUTILE FINGERTIPS CRAWLING FORWARD.
WHAT ARE YOU DOING IN MY GARDEN!?

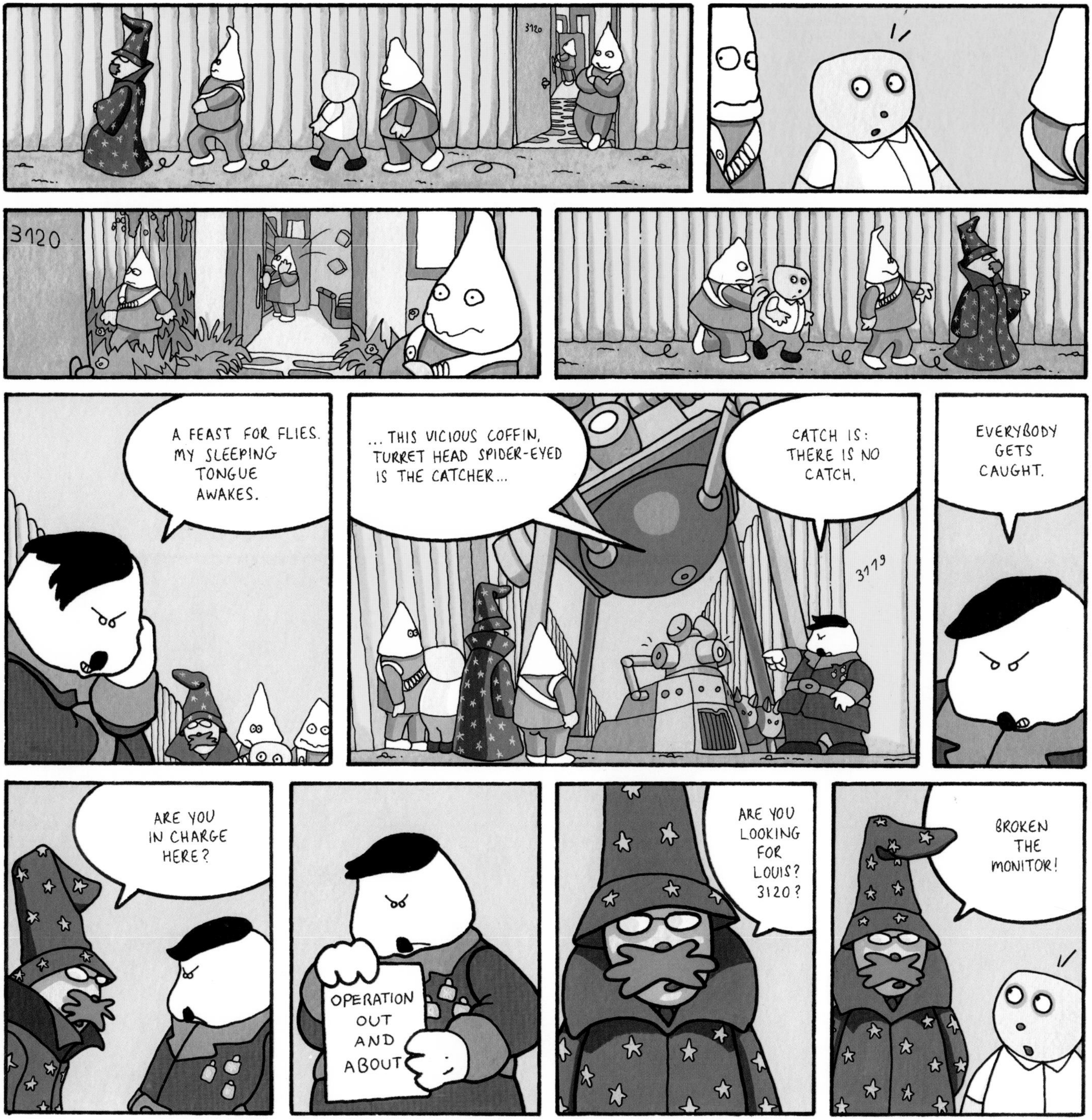
3120
3120
A FEAST FOR FLIES. MY SLEEPING TONGUE AWAKES.
... THIS VICIOUS COFFIN, TURRET HEAD SPIDER-EYED IS THE CATCHER...
CATCH IS: THERE IS NO CATCH.
3119
EVERYBODY GETS CAUGHT.
ARE YOU IN CHARGE HERE?
OPERATION OUT AND ABOUT
ARE YOU LOOKING FOR LOUIS? 3120?
BROKEN THE MONITOR!

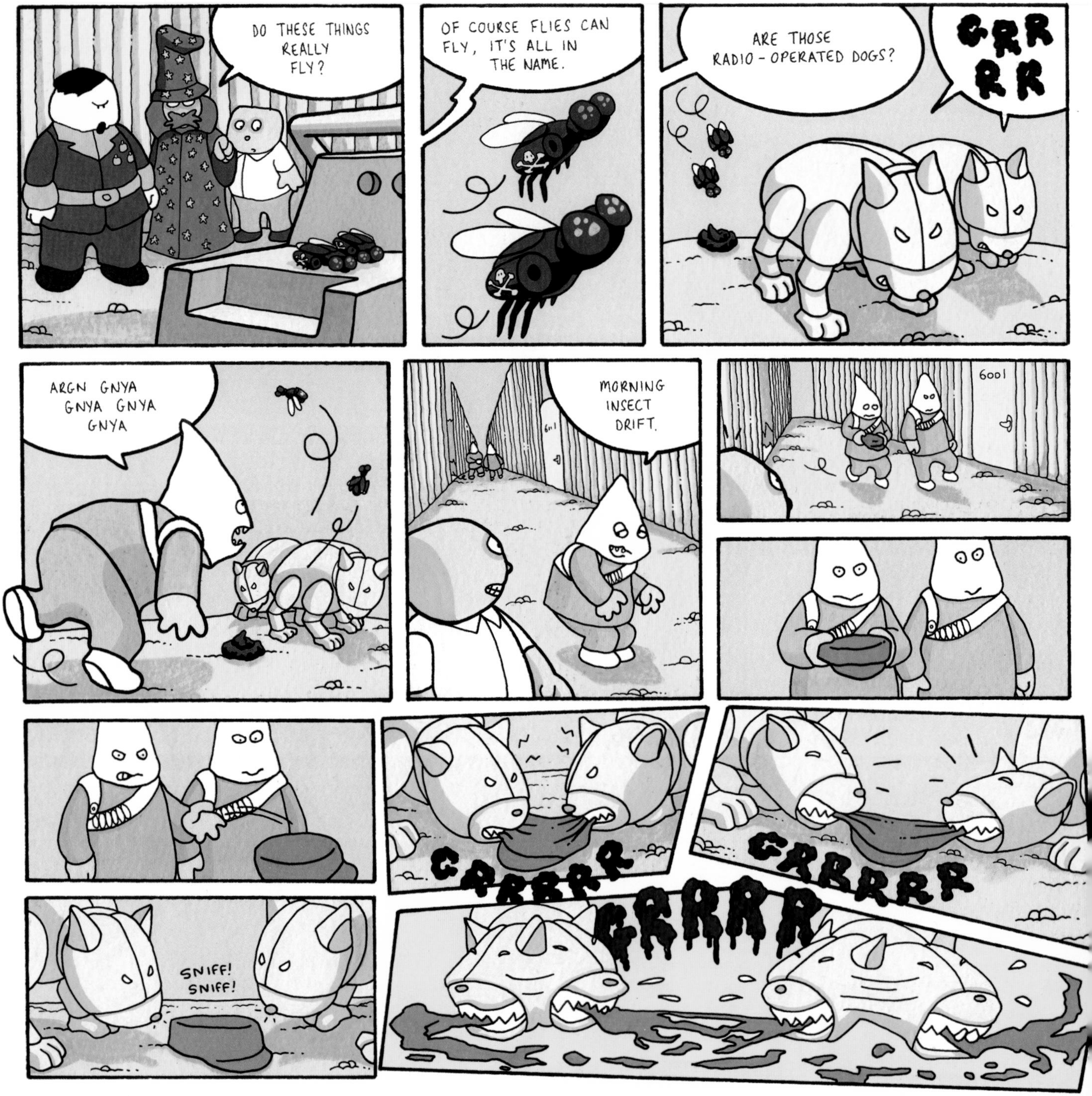
DO THESE THINGS REALLY FLY?
OF COURSE FLIES CAN FLY, IT'S ALL IN THE NAME.
ARE THOSE RADIO-OPERATED DOGS?
GRR RR
ARGN GNYA GNYA GNYA GNYA
MORNING INSECT DRIFT.
GRRRRR
GRRRRRR
SNIFF! SNIFF!
GRRRR

YOUR DOG DID IT!
DO YOU THINK YOU COULD DESCRIBE THE CULPRIT... ?
PICTORIALLY...
...

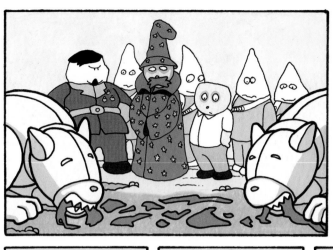

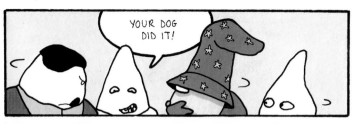

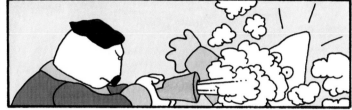

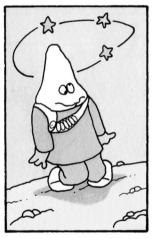

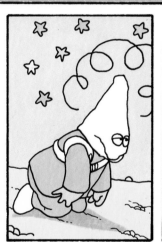

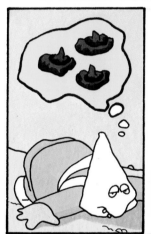

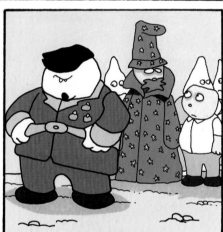

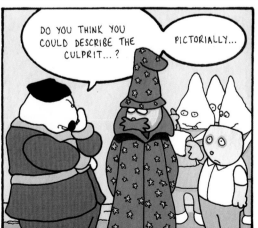

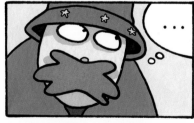

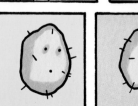

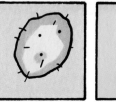

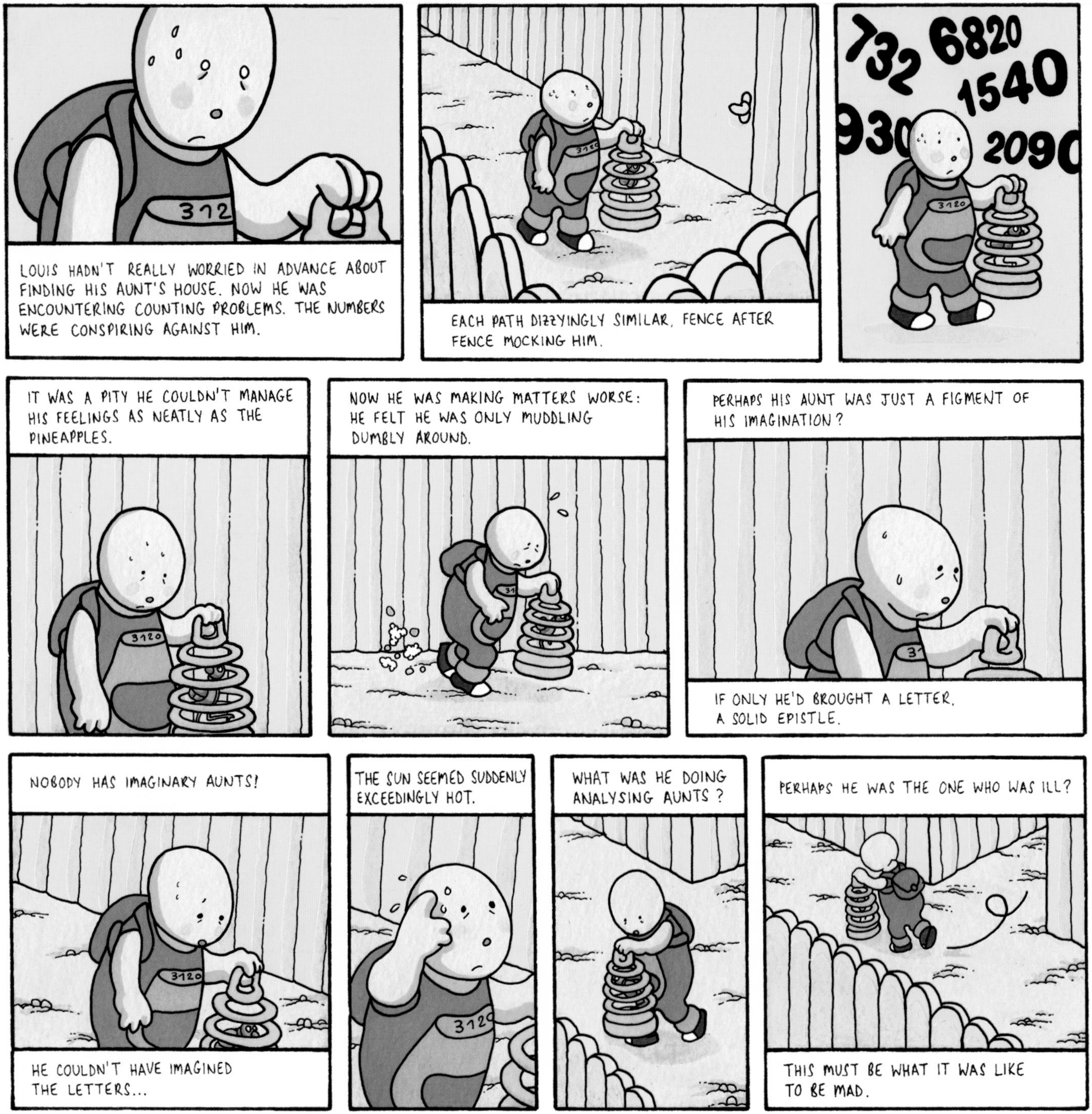
312
LOUIS HADN'T REALLY WORRIED IN ADVANCE ABOUT FINDING HIS AUNT'S HOUSE. NOW HE WAS ENCOUNTERING COUNTING PROBLEMS. THE NUMBERS WERE CONSPIRING AGAINST HIM.
EACH PATH DIZZYINGLY SIMILAR, FENCE AFTER FENCE MOCKING HIM.
732 6820
1540
930
2090
3120
IT WAS A PITY HE COULDN'T MANAGE HIS FEELINGS AS NEATLY AS THE PINEAPPLES.
3120
NOW HE WAS MAKING MATTERS WORSE: HE FELT HE WAS ONLY MUDDLING DUMBLY AROUND.
PERHAPS HIS AUNT WAS JUST A FIGMENT OF HIS IMAGINATION?
IF ONLY HE'D BROUGHT A LETTER. A SOLID EPISTLE.
NOBODY HAS IMAGINARY AUNTS!
3120
HE COULDN'T HAVE IMAGINED THE LETTERS...
THE SUN SEEMED SUDDENLY EXCEEDINGLY HOT.
WHAT WAS HE DOING ANALYSING AUNTS?
PERHAPS HE WAS THE ONE WHO WAS ILL?
THIS MUST BE WHAT IT WAS LIKE TO BE MAD.

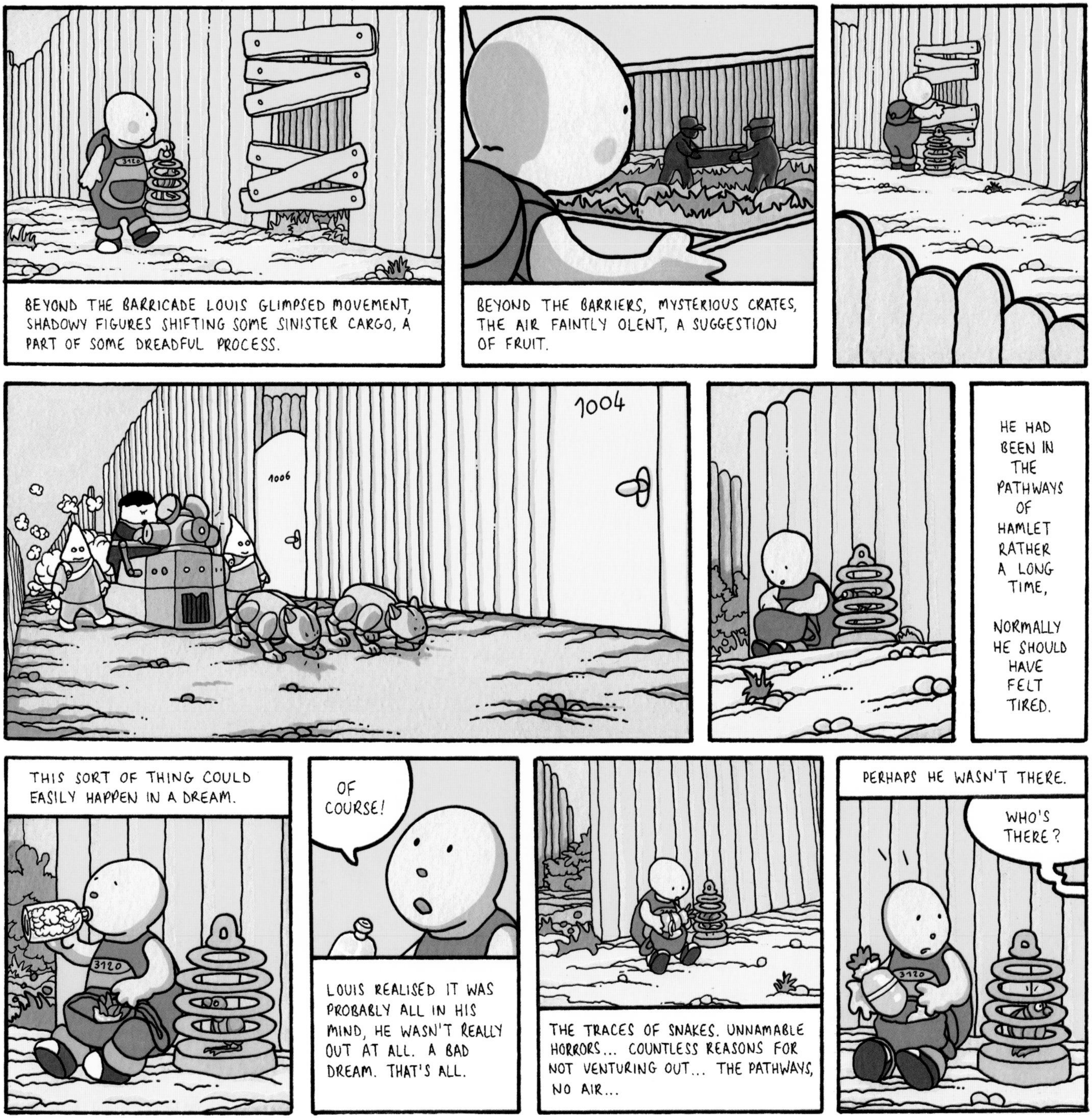
BEYOND THE BARRICADE LOUIS GLIMPSED MOVEMENT, SHADOWY FIGURES SHIFTING SOME SINISTER CARGO, A PART OF SOME DREADFUL PROCESS.
BEYOND THE BARRIERS, MYSTERIOUS CRATES, THE AIR FAINTLY OLENT, A SUGGESTION OF FRUIT.
1006
1004
HE HAD BEEN IN THE PATHWAYS OF HAMLET RATHER A LONG TIME,
NORMALLY HE SHOULD HAVE FELT TIRED.
THIS SORT OF THING COULD EASILY HAPPEN IN A DREAM.
OF COURSE!
LOUIS REALISED IT WAS PROBABLY ALL IN HIS MIND, HE WASN'T REALLY OUT AT ALL. A BAD DREAM. THAT'S ALL.
THE TRACES OF SNAKES. UNNAMABLE HORRORS... COUNTLESS REASONS FOR NOT VENTURING OUT... THE PATHWAYS, NO AIR...
PERHAPS HE WASN'T THERE.
WHO'S THERE?

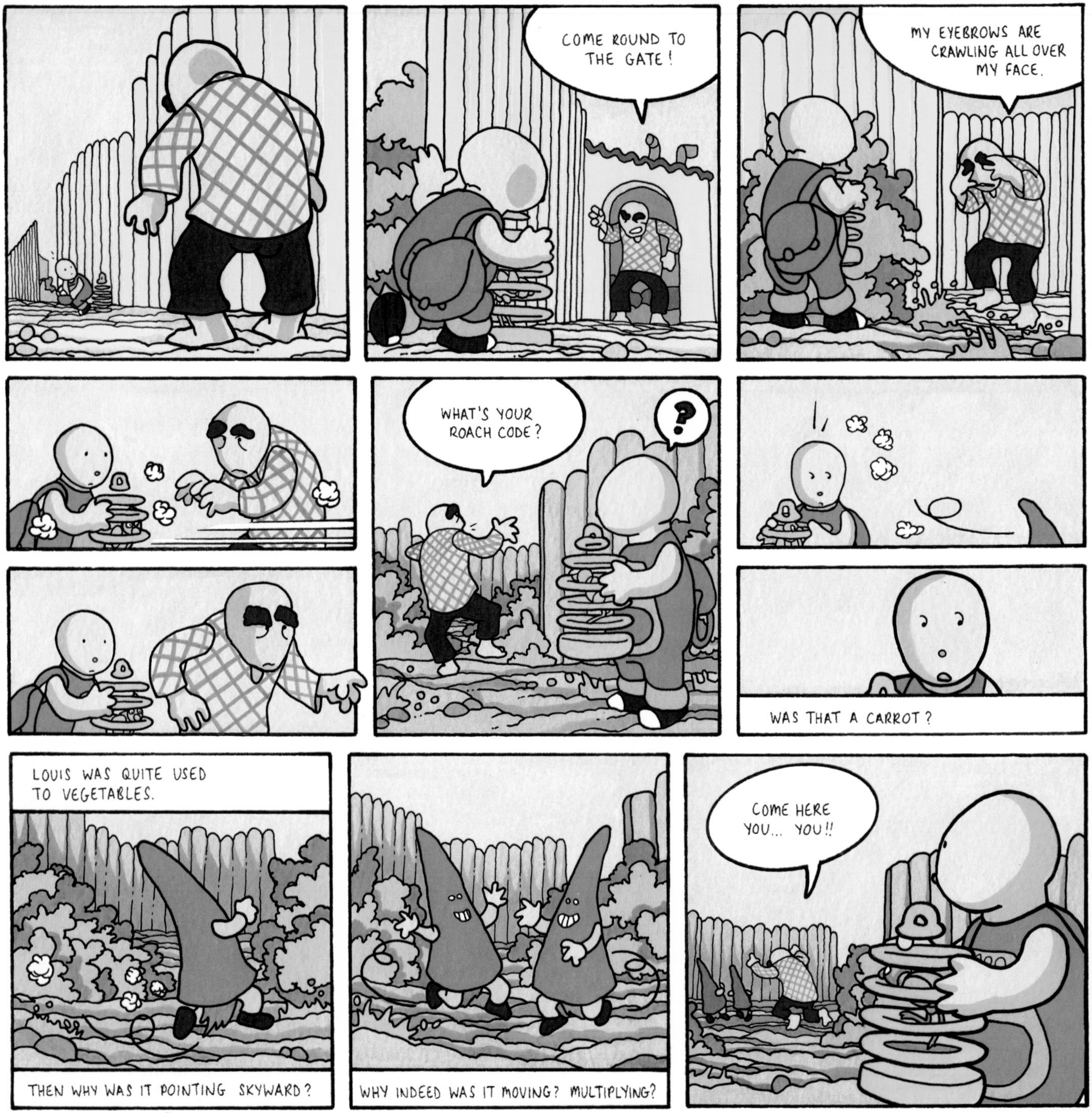

COME ROUND TO THE GATE!
MY EYEBROWS ARE CRAWLING ALL OVER MY FACE.
WHAT'S YOUR ROACH CODE?
?
WAS THAT A CARROT?
LOUIS WAS QUITE USED TO VEGETABLES.
THEN WHY WAS IT POINTING SKYWARD?
WHY INDEED WAS IT MOVING? MULTIPLYING?
COME HERE YOU... YOU!!

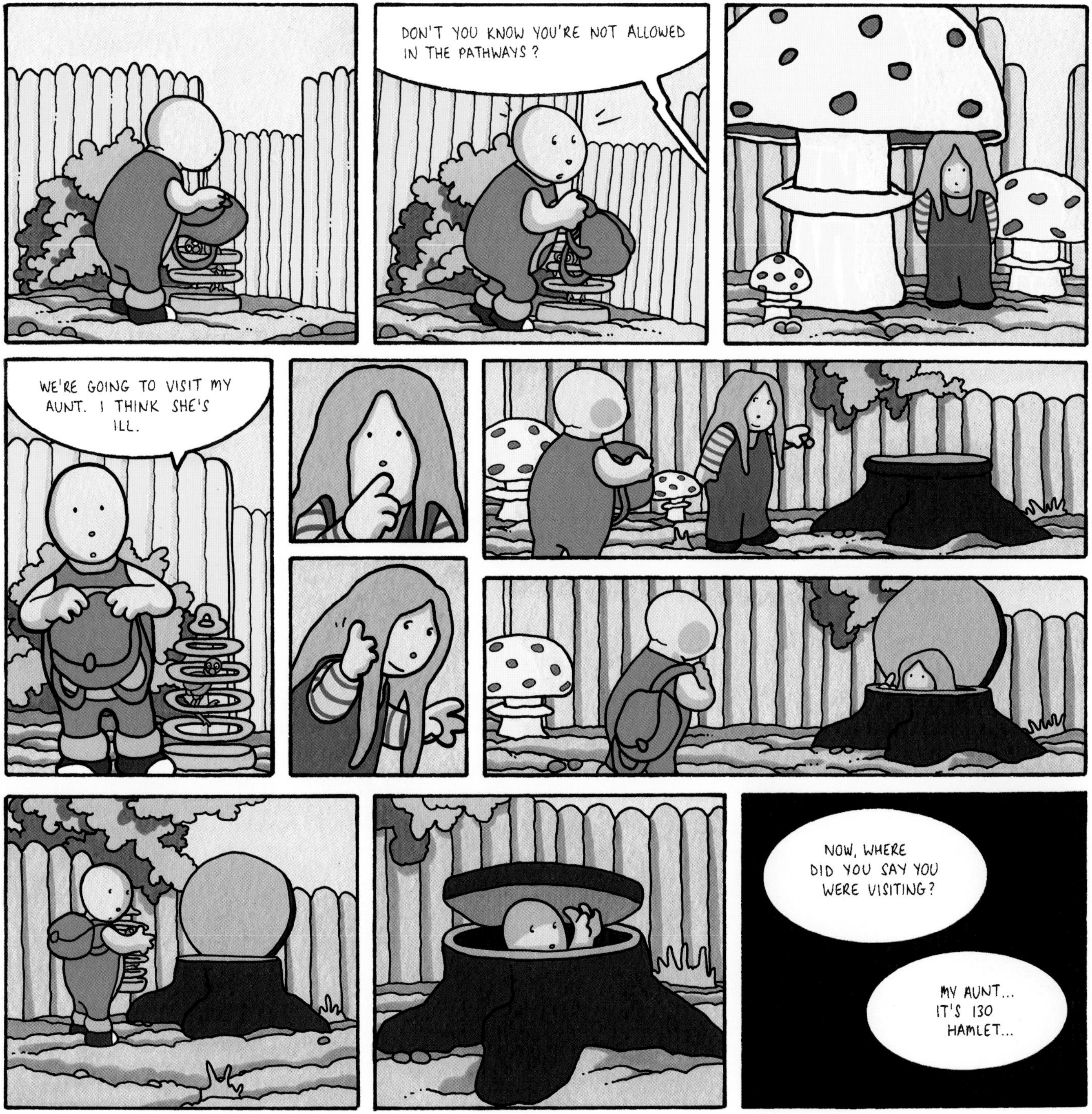
DON'T YOU KNOW YOU'RE NOT ALLOWED IN THE PATHWAYS?
WE'RE GOING TO VISIT MY AUNT. I THINK SHE'S ILL.
NOW, WHERE DID YOU SAY YOU WERE VISITING?
MY AUNT... IT'S 130 HAMLET...

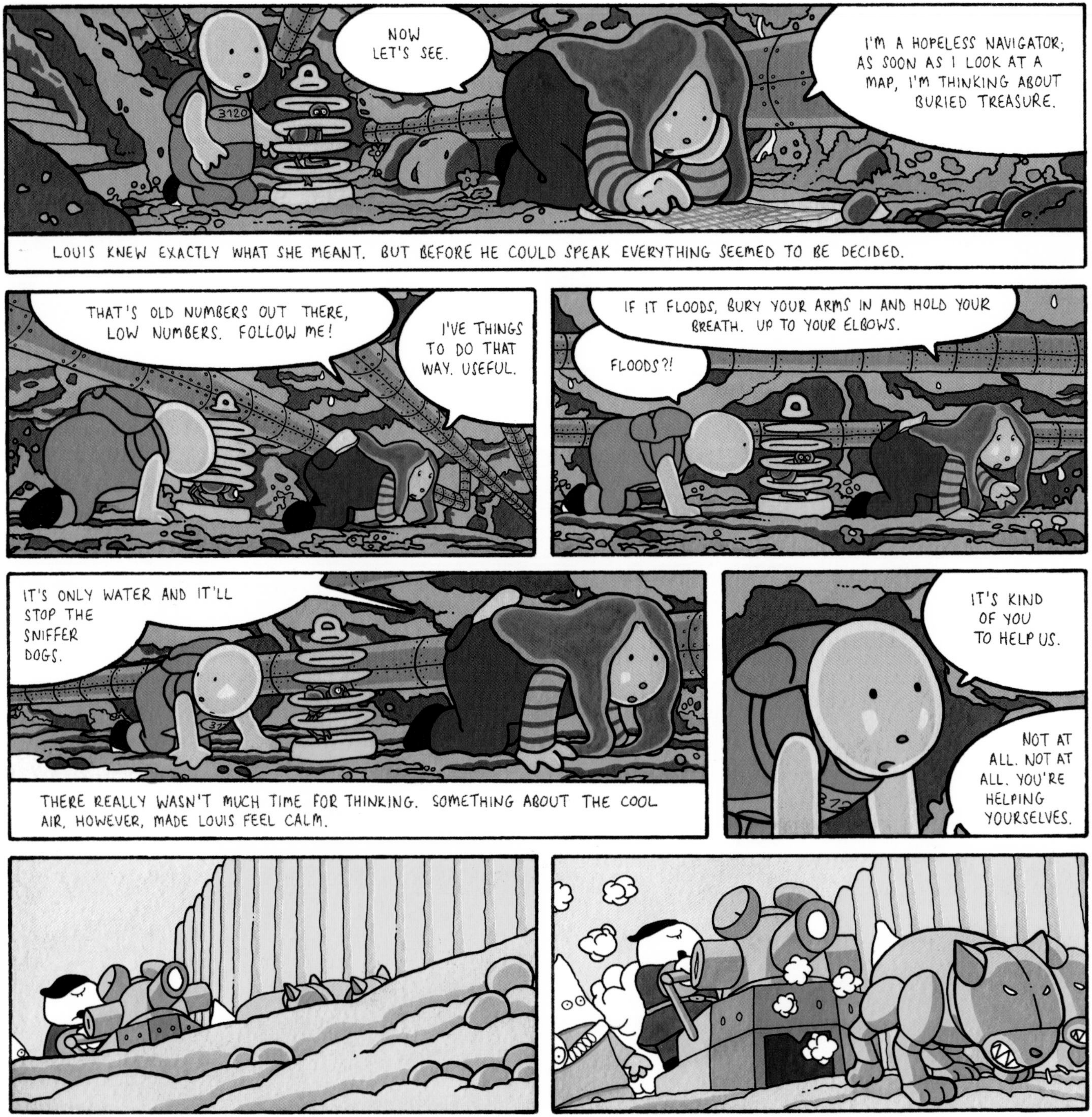
NOW LET'S SEE.
I'M A HOPELESS NAVIGATOR; AS SOON AS I LOOK AT A MAP, I'M THINKING ABOUT BURIED TREASURE.
LOUIS KNEW EXACTLY WHAT SHE MEANT. BUT BEFORE HE COULD SPEAK EVERYTHING SEEMED TO BE DECIDED.
THAT'S OLD NUMBERS OUT THERE, LOW NUMBERS. FOLLOW ME!
I'VE THINGS TO DO THAT WAY. USEFUL.
IF IT FLOODS, BURY YOUR ARMS IN AND HOLD YOUR BREATH. UP TO YOUR ELBOWS.
FLOODS?!
IT'S ONLY WATER AND IT'LL STOP THE SNIFFER DOGS.
THERE REALLY WASN'T MUCH TIME FOR THINKING. SOMETHING ABOUT THE COOL AIR, HOWEVER, MADE LOUIS FEEL CALM.
IT'S KIND OF YOU TO HELP US.
NOT AT ALL. NOT AT ALL. YOU'RE HELPING YOURSELVES.

The map reads: map of Hamlet

THANK YOU!

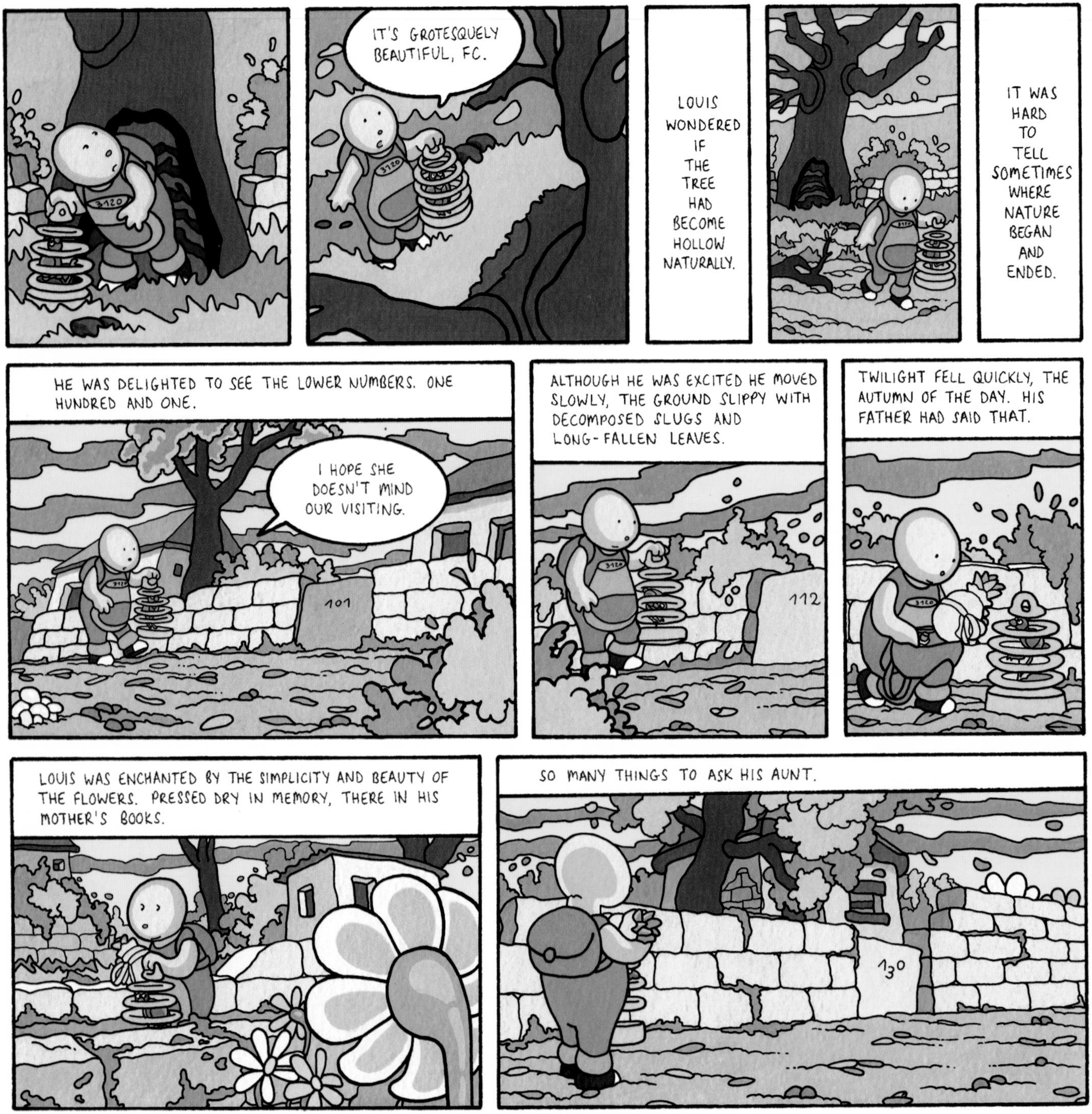
IT'S GROTESQUELY BEAUTIFUL, FC.
LOUIS WONDERED IF THE TREE HAD BECOME HOLLOW NATURALLY.
IT WAS HARD TO TELL SOMETIMES WHERE NATURE BEGAN AND ENDED.
HE WAS DELIGHTED TO SEE THE LOWER NUMBERS. ONE HUNDRED AND ONE.
I HOPE SHE DOESN'T MIND OUR VISITING.
101
ALTHOUGH HE WAS EXCITED HE MOVED SLOWLY, THE GROUND SLIPPY WITH DECOMPOSED SLUGS AND LONG-FALLEN LEAVES.
112
TWILIGHT FELL QUICKLY, THE AUTUMN OF THE DAY. HIS FATHER HAD SAID THAT.
LOUIS WAS ENCHANTED BY THE SIMPLICITY AND BEAUTY OF THE FLOWERS. PRESSED DRY IN MEMORY, THERE IN HIS MOTHER'S BOOKS.
SO MANY THINGS TO ASK HIS AUNT.
130

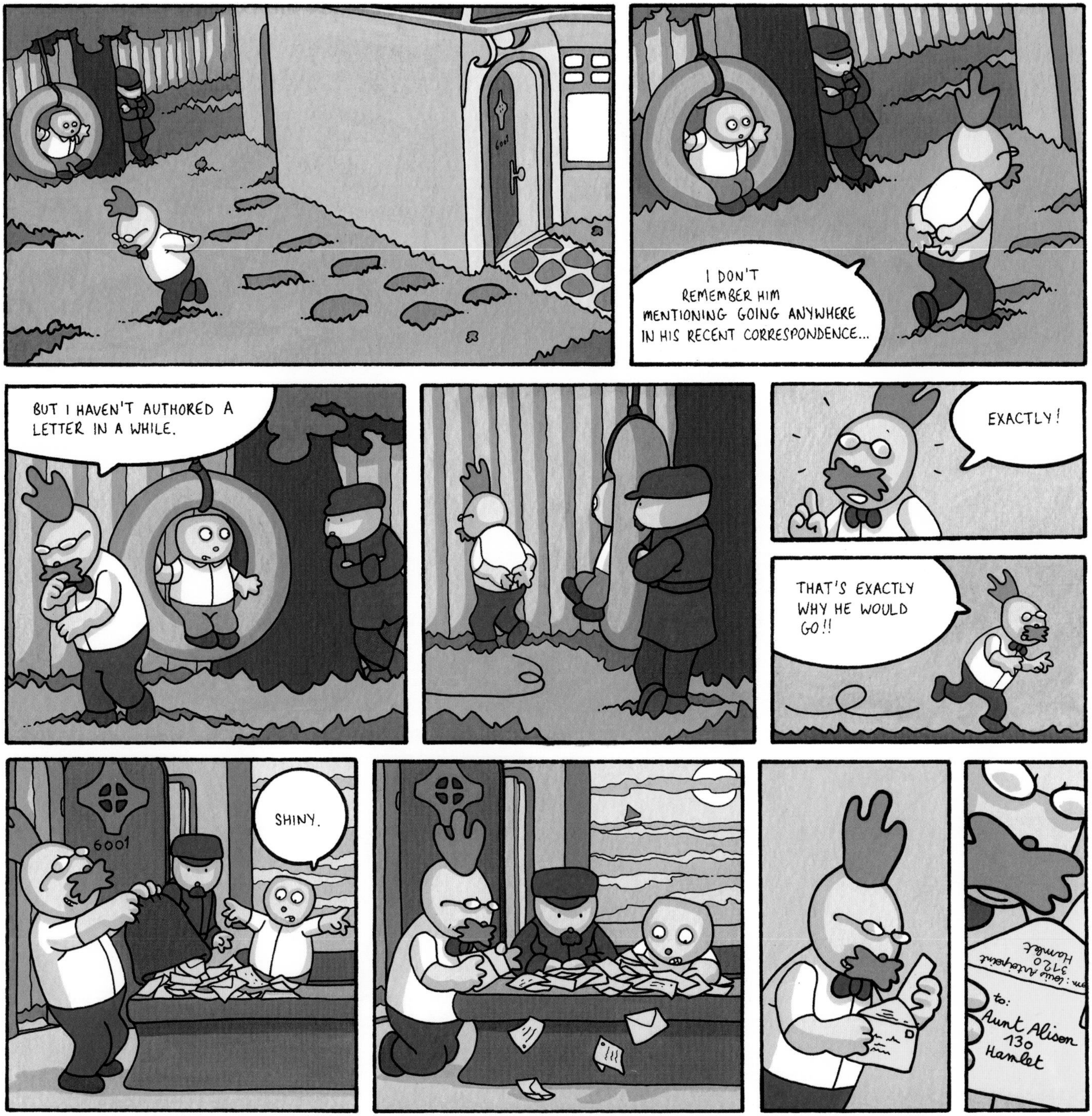
I DON'T REMEMBER HIM MENTIONING GOING ANYWHERE IN HIS RECENT CORRESPONDENCE...
BUT I HAVEN'T AUTHORED A LETTER IN A WHILE.
EXACTLY!
THAT'S EXACTLY WHY HE WOULD GO!!
6001
SHINY.
to:
Aunt Alison
130
Hamlet

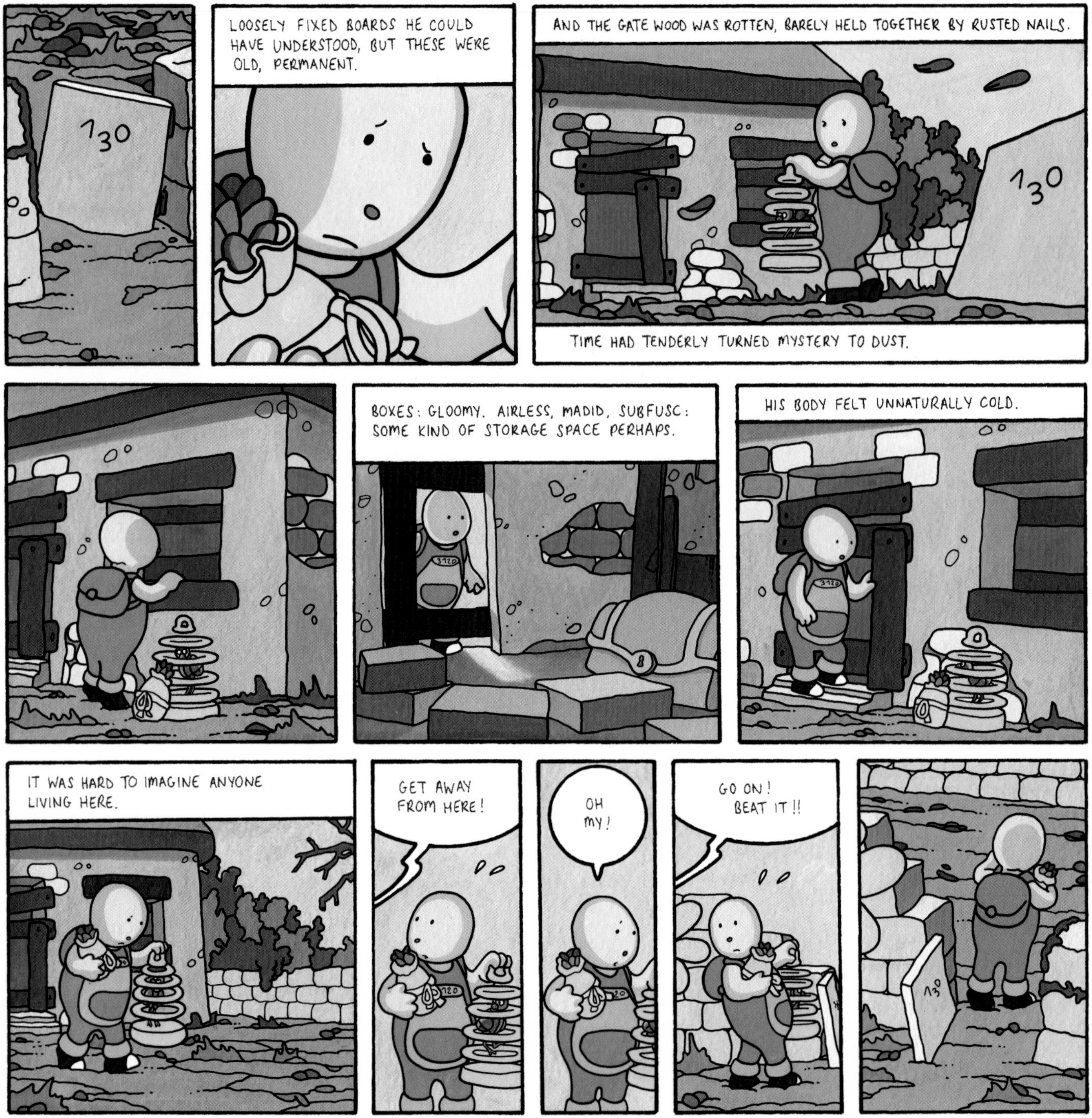
130
LOOSELY FIXED BOARDS HE COULD HAVE UNDERSTOOD, BUT THESE WERE OLD, PERMANENT.
AND THE GATE WOOD WAS ROTTEN, BARELY HELD TOGETHER BY RUSTED NAILS.
130
TIME HAD TENDERLY TURNED MYSTERY TO DUST.
BOXES: GLOOMY. AIRLESS, MADID, SUBFUSC: SOME KIND OF STORAGE SPACE PERHAPS.
HIS BODY FELT UNNATURALLY COLD.
IT WAS HARD TO IMAGINE ANYONE LIVING HERE.
GET AWAY FROM HERE!
OH MY!
GO ON! BEAT IT!!
130

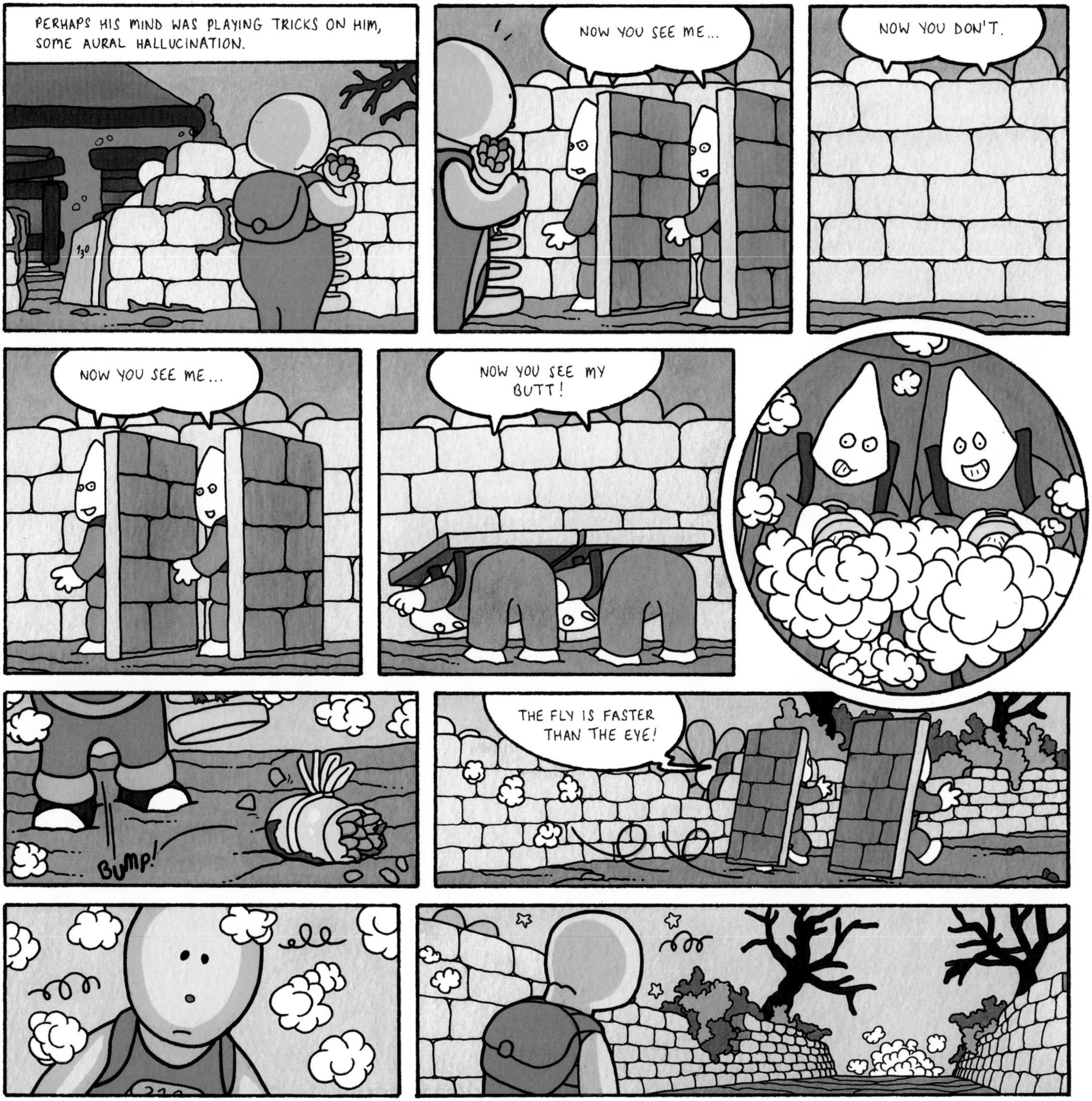
PERHAPS HIS MIND WAS PLAYING TRICKS ON HIM, SOME AURAL HALLUCINATION.
NOW YOU SEE ME...
NOW YOU DON'T.
NOW YOU SEE ME...
NOW YOU SEE MY BUTT!
BUMP!
THE FLY IS FASTER THAN THE EYE!

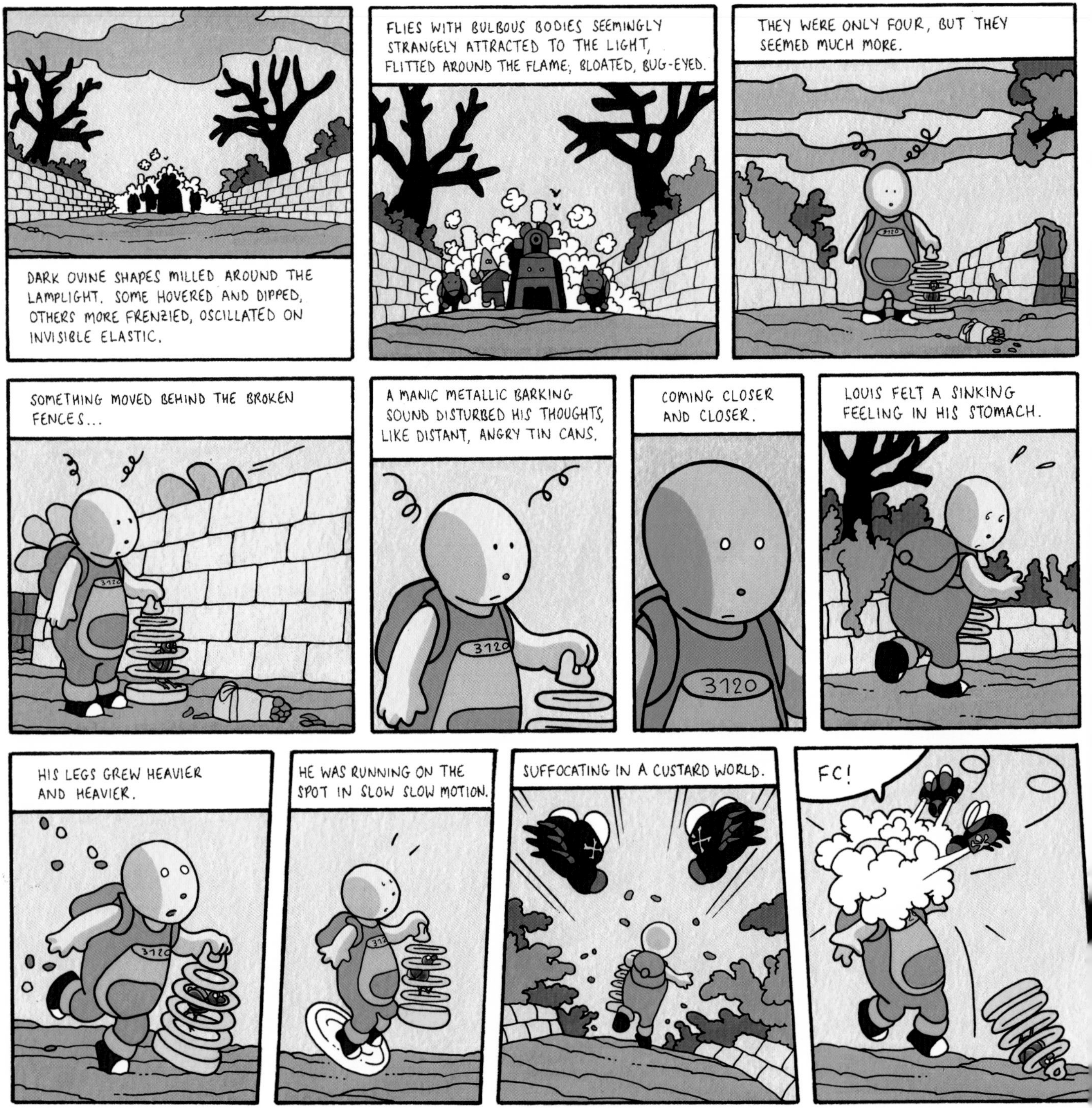
DARK OVINE SHAPES MILLED AROUND THE LAMPLIGHT. SOME HOVERED AND DIPPED, OTHERS MORE FRENZIED, OSCILLATED ON INVISIBLE ELASTIC.
FLIES WITH BULBOUS BODIES SEEMINGLY STRANGELY ATTRACTED TO THE LIGHT, FLITTED AROUND THE FLAME; BLOATED, BUG-EYED.
THEY WERE ONLY FOUR, BUT THEY SEEMED MUCH MORE.
3120
SOMETHING MOVED BEHIND THE BROKEN FENCES...
3120
A MANIC METALLIC BARKING SOUND DISTURBED HIS THOUGHTS, LIKE DISTANT, ANGRY TIN CANS.
3120
COMING CLOSER AND CLOSER.
3120
LOUIS FELT A SINKING FEELING IN HIS STOMACH.
HIS LEGS GREW HEAVIER AND HEAVIER.
3120
HE WAS RUNNING ON THE SPOT IN SLOW SLOW MOTION.
SUFFOCATING IN A CUSTARD WORLD.
FC!

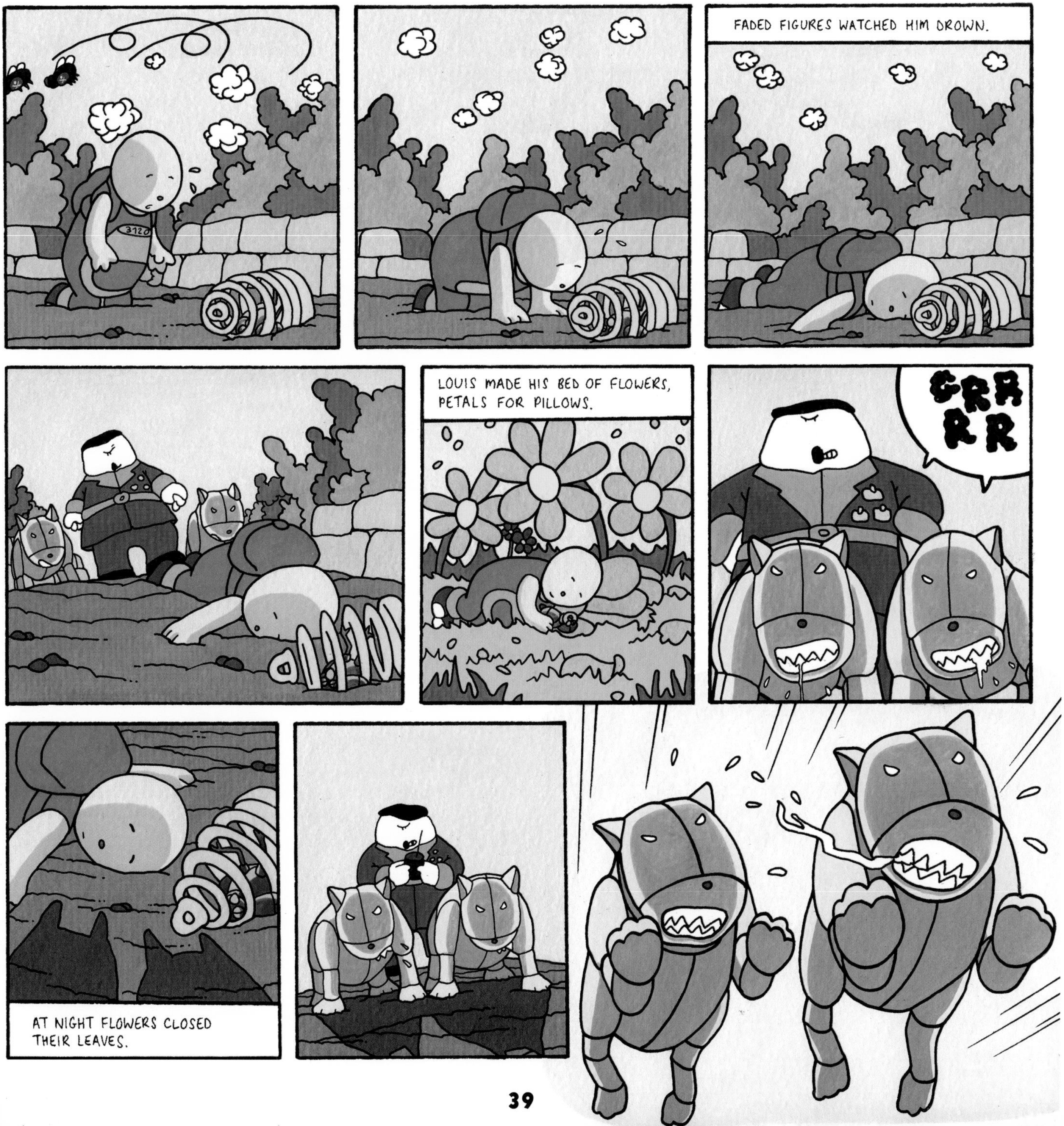
3120
FADED FIGURES WATCHED HIM DROWN.
LOUIS MADE HIS BED OF FLOWERS, PETALS FOR PILLOWS.
GRR RR
AT NIGHT FLOWERS CLOSED THEIR LEAVES.

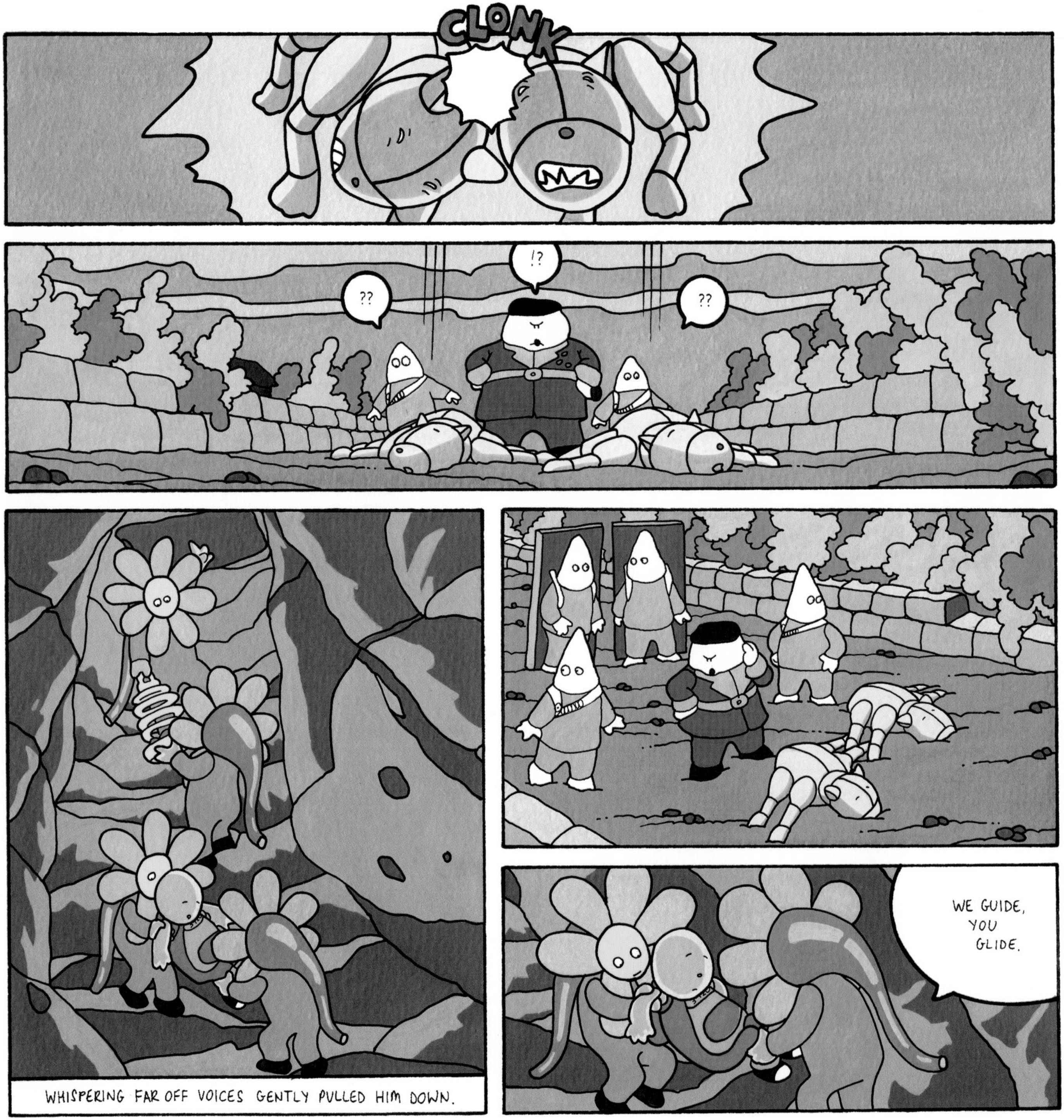

CLONK
??
!?
??
WHISPERING FAR OFF VOICES GENTLY PULLED HIM DOWN.
WE GUIDE, YOU GLIDE.

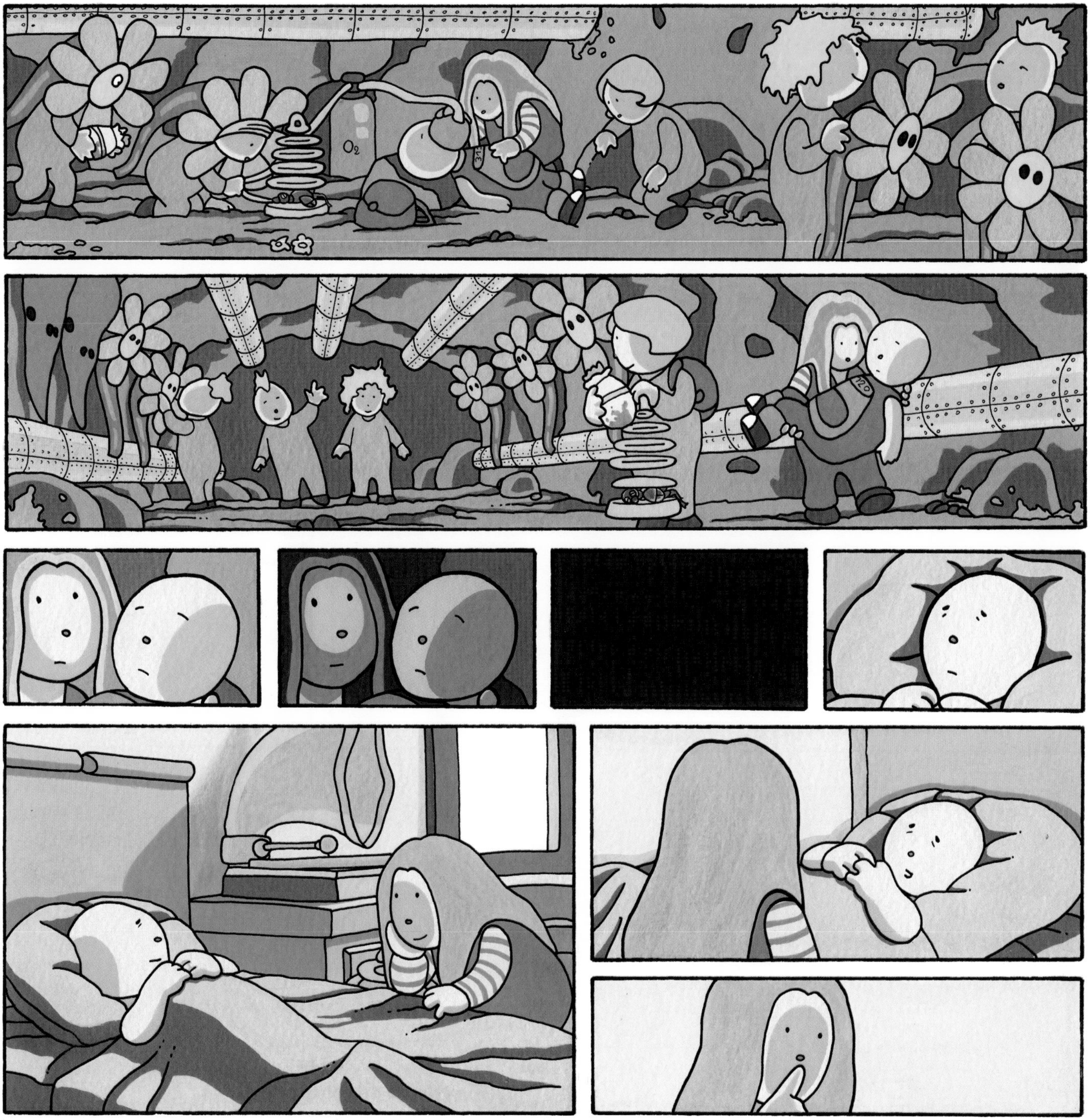
O2

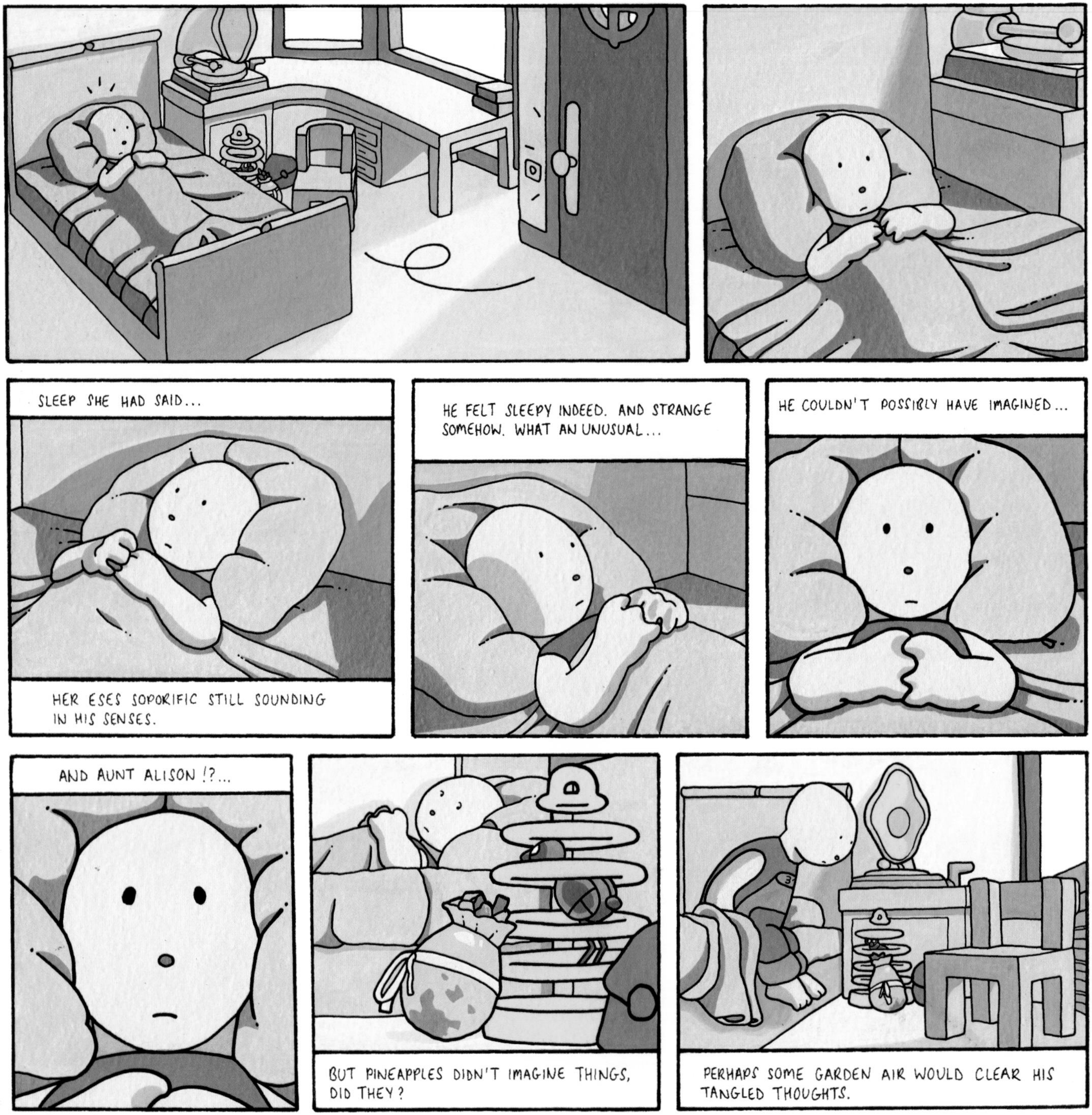
SLEEP SHE HAD SAID...
HER ESES SOPORIFIC STILL SOUNDING IN HIS SENSES.
HE FELT SLEEPY INDEED. AND STRANGE SOMEHOW. WHAT AN UNUSUAL...
HE COULDN'T POSSIBLY HAVE IMAGINED...
AND AUNT ALISON !?...
BUT PINEAPPLES DIDN'T IMAGINE THINGS, DID THEY?
PERHAPS SOME GARDEN AIR WOULD CLEAR HIS TANGLED THOUGHTS.

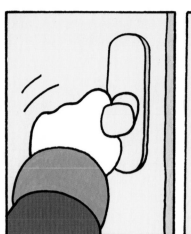

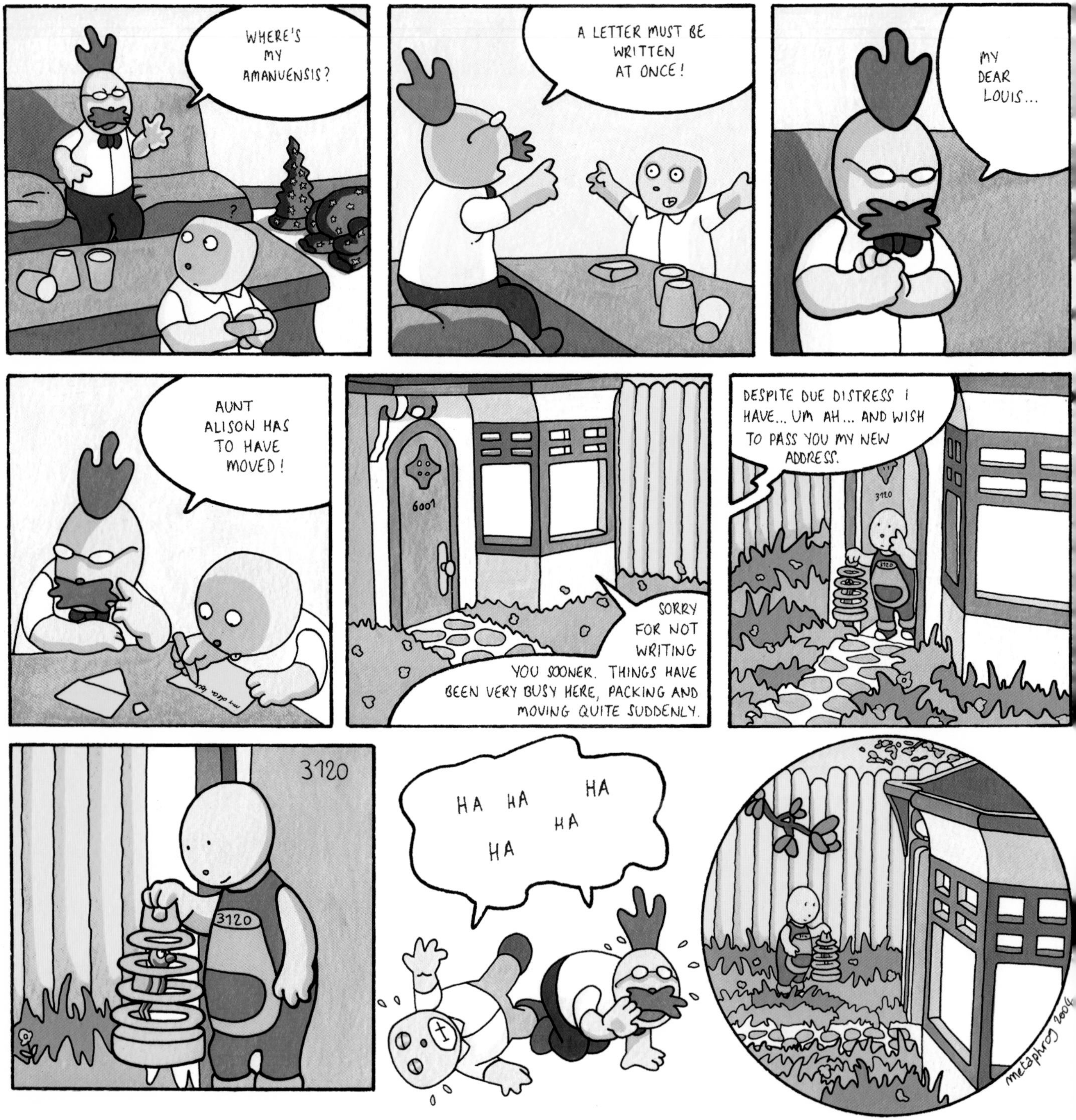
WHERE'S MY AMANUENSIS?
A LETTER MUST BE WRITTEN AT ONCE!
MY DEAR LOUIS...
AUNT ALISON HAS TO HAVE MOVED!
6001
SORRY FOR NOT WRITING YOU SOONER. THINGS HAVE BEEN VERY BUSY HERE, PACKING AND MOVING QUITE SUDDENLY.
DESPITE DUE DISTRESS I HAVE... UM AH... AND WISH TO PASS YOU MY NEW ADDRESS.
3120
3120
3120
HA HA HA HA HA
metaphrog 2004

Thanks to our sponsors:

A1 Books & Comics 31- 35 Parnie Street Glasgow G1 5RJ Tel: 0141 552 6692 - 28 Argyle Street Glasgow Tel: 0141 226 5414 www.A1comics.com - **Abstract Sprocket** 29 St Benedict's Street Norwich NR2 4PF Tel: 01603 624410 www.abstractsprocket.com - **Café Gandolfi** 61 Albion Street Glasgow G1 Tel: 0141 552 6813 - **Grassroots** 20 Woodlands Road Charing X Glasgow G3 6UR Tel: 0141 353 3278 - **John Moffat Print & Design** Green City 23 Fleming Street Glasgow G31 Tel: 0141 556 2382 sales@print-design.freeserve.co.uk - **King Tuts Wah Wah Hut** 272 St Vincent Street Glasgow G2 5RL Tel: 0141 221 5279 - **Merchant City Music** 7 Garth Street Glasgow G1 1UT Tel: 0141 552 6290 Fax: 0141 552 4148 www.GuitarStrings.co.uk - **mono** Unit 12 Kings Court King Street Glasgow G1 5RB - **Nice'n'Sleazy** 421 Sauchiehall Street Glasgow Tel: 0141 333 0900 - **Northern Lightz** P.O. Box 25285 Glasgow G2 6WD Tel: 0141 221 5888 www.northernlightz.com - **Quigg's of Glasgow** 7-11 Parnie Street Glasgow G1 5RJ Tel: 0141 552 6823 - **rubadub** 35 Howard Street Glasgow G1 4BA Tel: 0141 221 9650 info@rubadub.co.uk - **Variety Bar** 401 Sauchiehall Street Glasgow G2 Tel: 0141 332 4449